HOMOSEXUALITY

**Lesbians and Gay Men
in Society, History and Literature**

THE HOMOSEXUAL
EMANCIPATION MOVEMENT
IN GERMANY

James D. Steakley

ARNO PRESS
A NEW YORK TIMES COMPANY
New York — 1975

Editorial Supervision: LESLIE PARR

———◆———

First publication 1975 by Arno Press Inc.

Copyright © 1975 by James D. Steakley

HOMOSEXUALITY: Lesbians and Gay Men in
Society, History and Literature
ISBN for complete set: 0-405-07348-8
See last pages of this volume for titles.

Manufactured in the United States of America

———◆———

Library of Congress Cataloging in Publication Data

Steakley, James D
    The homosexual emancipation movement in Germany.

    (Homosexuality)
    1. Gay liberation movement--Germany--History--
Addresses, essays, lectures. 2. Gay liberation move-
ment--Germany--Sources. I. Title. II. Series.
HQ76.8.G4S8   301.41'57'0943   75-13728
ISBN 0-405-07366-6

PREFACE

My research into the history of the German homosexual emancipation movement began three years ago as a background study
for a larger project on the image of male homosexuality in the
fiction of the Wilhelmine era. It seemed that a proper evalua-
tion of the dated and occasionally bizarre portrayal of homosexuals in period fiction would be impossible without some knowledge
of the social and historical context in which it was written.
Later, I was encouraged by members of the *Body Politic* collective
to write up my findings for publication and also to treat post-
Wilhelmine developments, and this book is an expanded and revised
version of three articles which appeared in that journal.

My approach to the subject still shows something of a literary bias: the reader will find that medical, sexological, and
psychological writings have been largely ignored, although they
had a great influence upon (and were in turn influenced by) the
German movement. I lack the qualifications to deal with this
material, and I have likewise left the topic of lesbianism virtually untouched. An anthology of German writings on feminism and
lesbianism from the turn of the century is being issued by Arno
Press simultaneously with this book, and these materials will
hopefully stimulate future research.

Readers who find that this history ends on a rather negative
note should be aware that the German movement re-emerged almost

immediately after the collapse of Nazism; more information on the post-war German movement appears in issue #13 of *The Body Politic*. Moreover, the movement had taken root in Switzerland in the late twenties and continued operations there through the years of the Third Reich: thus the movement has an uninterrupted history stretching back to 1897.

I would like to thank Ed Drucker, Wayne Dynes, Richard Hall, Manfred Herzer, Warren Johansson, Jonathan Katz, John Lauritsen, Richard Mehringer, Bernd Metz, Kenneth Popert, Joseph Savago, John J. Shafer, Jr., David Thorstad, and Ian Young for providing me with leads, information, books, translations, constructive criticism, and encouragement. My thanks also go to the *Body Politic* collective and Leslie Parr of Arno Press for their patience. Finally, the book is dedicated to Friedhelm Krey.

New York City

May 1, 1975

CONTENTS

LIST OF ILLUSTRATIONS

ILLUSTRATION SOURCES

Figures 1, 2, 8, 13, 16, 17, 18, and 19, Magnus Hirschfeld, *Geschlechtskunde*, vol. 4 (Stuttgart: Julius Püttmann, 1930); 20, *ibid.*, vol. 1 (1926); 3, *Jahrbuch für sexuelle Zwischenstufen* XXII (1922); 5, 6, and 7, *Jugend*; 9, Benedict Friedländer, *Die Liebe Platons im Lichte der modernen Biologie* (Berlin-Treptow: Bernhard Zack, 1909); 10, Elisár von Kupffer, *Heiland Kunst: Ein Gespräch in Florenz* (Jena: Hermann Costenoble, 1907); 11, private collection; 12, Arthur Kracke (ed.), *Freideutsche Jugend* (Jena: Eugen Diederichs, 1913); 14, Kurt Hiller, *Leben gegen die Zeit*, vol. 1, *Logos* (Reinbek bei Hamburg: Rowohlt, 1969); 15, Leo Schidrowitz (ed.), *Sittengeschichte des Lasters* (Vienna: Verlag für Kulturforschung, 1927); 21, *Anthropos* I (1934).

CHAPTER I

THE END OF INVISIBILITY

1862 - 1870

In 1862, a talented lawyer named Jean Baptiste von Schweitzer
(1834-1875) joined the workers' movement in his native Hessen.
A writer of some note--he was later to become editor of the journal *Sozialdemokrat* (Social Democrat) and the author of a number
of valuable works of socialist propaganda--Schweitzer was welcomed
as a valuable addition to the growing movement. If his new colleagues were thoroughly acquainted with his past, they may have
known that in 1858 Schweitzer had published a four-act comedy
entitled *Alcibiades oder Bilder aus Hellas* (Alcibiades, or Pictures from Hellas), a play which contained some strikingly real-
istic references to Greek love. But Schweitzer was noted primarily as a writer who could depict the social life of various
classes with keen insight: it was his novel *Lucinde oder Kapital
und Arbeit* (Lucinde, or Capital and Labor) which had first brought
him to the attention of the movement's leader, Ferdinand Lassalle,
and Schweitzer's propriety was unchallenged.

In August of that year, two elderly ladies enjoying a quiet
stroll through the public park of Mannheim came upon Schweitzer
and an unidentified young man in a highly compromising situation.

Justice was swift: Schweitzer appeared in court on September 5,

and he was found guilty of public indecency and sentenced to two

weeks in jail. There were, of course, further repercussions:

Schweitzer was disbarred from the practice of law, and the career

he had planned as a political organizer was clearly in trouble.

Looking back on these events some fifty years later, the

great Social Democratic leader August Bebel observed:

> The offense would have been punished far more severely if
> the boy involved could have been apprehended. The attempt
> failed. But other boys of whom Schweitzer had made the
> same demand were indeed found. He was thereupon convicted.
> Out of zeal to clear Schweitzer's name, an attempt was
> made to prove his innocence. In the interest of historical
> truth, such efforts should be eschewed. And no matter
> how freely one regards same-sex love, it was clearly
> dishonorable to seek its gratification in broad daylight,
> in a public park, and with a school-age boy. (1)

The disapproval expressed by Bebel was voiced in even stronger

terms by many of Schweitzer's working-class colleagues.

In 1863, Lassalle founded the Universal German Workingmen's

Association, and Schweitzer's attempt to join the Frankfurt

chapter was hotly contested by some members. Lassalle personally

intervened on behalf of Schweitzer and wrote to him:

> Assuming that what the newspapers said at the time about
> the reason for your conviction was true, I know one
> thing: the regrettable and, to my taste, incomprehensible
> inclination imputed to you is one of those trespasses
> which have absolutely nothing to do with a man's political
> character. Such a reaction toward a man of your character
> and intelligence proves only how confused and philistine
> the political concepts of our people still are. . . . (2)

With the backing of Lassalle, Schweitzer (who continued to protest

his innocence) was duly admitted to the Association. He rose to

the presidency of the organization in 1867, and on September 7
he was elected to the Reichstag of the North German Confederation.

To a very appreciable extent, the continuation of Schweitzer's
political career was due to the liberalism of the leading socialist of the times--a role to be assumed for the succeeding generation by August Bebel. The opposition of Schweitzer's Frankfurt
colleagues, however, points to the fact that socialist opinion
was by no means undivided. During the decades to come, when the
Social Democratic Party clearly emerged as the champion of homosexual emancipation, the subject would remain controversial within
the ranks of the German left.

At the same time that Schweitzer was undergoing the ordeal
of public exposure in court, another German lawyer was actively
seeking exposure and entering a preemptory plea of innocence
before a tribunal of a different sort--his family. In the second
half of 1862, Karl Heinrich Ulrichs (1825-1895) wrote a series
of letters to his family in which he forthrightly confronted them
with his homosexuality and challenged them to understand and
accept his sexual proclivities.[3] In a postscript to the second
of these letters, written as a circular to eight relatives, Ulrichs gave notice that he planned to launch an educational campaign, an undertaking "of the utmost necessity," by issuing a
series of writings on the subject.

Over the course of the next seventeen years, Ulrichs wrote

4

and printed at his own expense twelve books which bore the
collective title *Forschungen über das Räthsel der mannmännlichen Liebe* (Researches on the Riddle of Love between Men).
The historical importance of these books was later described
by John Addington Symonds:

> It can hardly be said that inverted sexuality received
> a serious and sympathetic treatment until. . .Ulrichs
> began his long warfare against what he considered to be
> a prejudice and ignorance upon a matter of the greatest
> moment. . . . (4)

Ulrichs took up the battle for homosexual emancipation with tremendous optimism. In the first of his books, *Vindex* (Vindicator,
1864), he wrote: "It was given to the two preceding centuries
to do away with the persecution of witchcraft and heresy. It
remains for our century, hopefully even our decade, to eliminate
the persecution of love between men."[5] He clearly recognized
that he could not press his cause to success single-handedly;
at the close of his third book, *Vindicta* (Staff of Freedom,
1864), he appealed to his fellows: "We should and must come
forward as homosexuals [*Urninge*]. We will win our place in
human society only if we do so--otherwise never." Ulrichs also
announced in *Vindicta* his intention to submit a motion to the
Congress of German Jurists, petitioning it to use its influence
to bring about a revision of the various German penal codes so
that "the inborn love for persons of the male sex be punishable
only under the same provisions which apply to love for persons
of the female sex."[6]

This plan was carried out the following year, but larger events now forced Ulrichs into an active political role. Ulrichs had written his first five books in his native Hanover, one of four German states (of twenty-five) which did not penalize homosexual acts. In Prussia, on the other hand, Paragraph 143 of the penal code punished homosexual offenses by imprisonment for up to four years. After Bismarck's victory in the Austro-Prussian War of 1866, Ulrichs had every reason to fear that the Prussian code would be extended to Hanover. (It was, in 1869.) He became an anti-Prussian agitator and was sentenced to one year in prison for his political activities. His house was searched for incriminating materials by the police, who instead discovered an enormous correspondence with homosexuals in various countries. After his release from prison Ulrichs quickly relocated to Bavaria, another of the states which did not penalize homosexuality.

Here he was within striking distance of the Congress of German Jurists, which held a convention in Munich on August 29, 1867. Ulrichs appeared at the convention to protest its refusal to consider the motion he had submitted two years earlier. He began a speech in which he pointed out that extant laws were based on a fundamental misunderstanding of the nature of homosexuality and had the effect of subjecting an innocent minority to untold persecutions. At this point, Ulrichs was shouted down by the shocked jurists; the efforts of the chairman to restore order were to no avail, and Ulrichs left the platform.

Considerably disheartened, Ulrichs returned to his writing.
In addition to his expertise in law and theology, he was widely
read in such fields as mathematics, archeology, and the natural
sciences. Fluent in a number of languages, Ulrichs was considered
one of the foremost Latinists of his time. After studying at
the universities of Göttingen and Berlin, Ulrichs had briefly
pursued a career as a civil servant in the Hanoverian judicial
system but had voluntarily retired at an early age in order to
pursue his scholarly interests.

1867 brought the publication of his single most important
work, *Memnon,* which bore the subtitle "The Sexual Nature of the
Man-Loving Uranian; Somatic-Psychic Hermaphroditism." This was
the first book which Ulrichs issued under his own name; as a concession to his relatives he had published his first five works
under the pseudonym Numa Numantius. *Memnon* offered a comprehensive review of Ulrichs' theory of homosexuality, and he brought
his formidable learning to bear upon the subject; the theory is
far too complex to be treated in detail here.[7]

In brief, Ulrichs advanced the notion that the male homosexual is a type of androgyne--specifically, a female soul con-
fined in a male body. Ulrichs was guided in his theorizing by
the mystical notion of metempsychosis *(Seelenwanderung)*, but he
was also familiar with the recent discoveries of embryology
concerning the lack of gender differentiation in human embryos.
He was intrigued by the existence of hermaphrodites and spoke of a

Karl Heinrich Ulrichs

Zwischenstufe (intermediate stage) between the sexes. Ulrichs'
theory, which he had expounded in a rudimentary form in his
letters of 1862, could easily account for both male and female
homosexuals, who constituted a "third sex." In *Formatrix*
(Creating Nature, 1864), Ulrichs grappled with the even greater
riddle of bisexuality.[8] The conclusion of Ulrichs' theories,
which ran counter to mainstream forensic medicine, was that
homosexuals do not choose their orientation or fall into it as
a form of vice. Rather, Ulrichs viewed homosexuality as a congenital anomaly, comparable to left-handedness--a minority trait,
to be sure, but neither contagious nor evil. Hence it was cruel
and pointless to attempt to coerce homosexuals to change by legal
or moral pressures.

Ulrichs' writings were not widely circulated and produced
virtually no support among contemporary homosexuals. His only
immediate contribution to the slowly emerging homosexual subculture of Western Europe was the name he coined, *Uranier* or
Urning (Uranian in English, *uraniste* in French). Based on
Plato's *Symposium,* in which the patron goddess of men who love
other men is identified as Aphrodite Urania, this word enjoyed
wide use up to World War I. Ulrichs' praxis was so far ahead
of his times that it left him totally isolated, but his theory
fell upon fertile ground within the scholarly community. To
cite but one of the scientists who were stimulated by Ulrichs'
concepts, Richard von Krafft-Ebing had this to say in a letter:

> The study of your writings on love between men has
> greatly interested me. . . . From the day--I believe
> it was in 1866--when you sent me your writings, I have
> turned my full attention to the subject, which at that
> time was equally puzzling and interesting to me: and
> it was solely the acquaintance with your writings which
> led me to studies in this most important area. . . . (9)

Another scientist who was acquainted with Ulrichs' work, Carl

von Westphal, published in 1869 what stands as the first psychi-

atric study of homosexuality.

Basing his conclusions on case histories of a lesbian and

a (heterosexual) male transvestite who had come afoul of the law,

Westphal declared that certain cases of "contrary sexual feeling"

(conträre Sexualempfindung) were a form of congenital psychopath-

ology, not acquired vice. He averred that homosexuality

> occurs more frequently than is realized, and it is a
> duty. . .to turn our attention to this subject. Should
> Paragraph 143 of the penal code be repealed and the
> specter of prison no longer appear as a threat to the
> confession of perverse inclinations, such cases will
> certainly come to the attention of doctors--in whose
> area they belong--in greater numbers. (10)

Westphal's progressive attitude toward law reform was neatly

balanced against what has aptly been termed an almost "imperial-

istic" expansion of psychiatry's interests.[11] At the time he

wrote his article on homosexuality, Westphal was emerging as

the foremost exponent of non-restraint in the treatment of psycho-

tics and eliminating asylums in favor of ambulatory clinics.

Westphal's liberal approach, the prototype of virtually every

form of clinical therapy developed in the past century, went

hand-in-hand with the redefinition of countless forms of malaise

and deviance (including homosexuality) as pathologies, thus
establishing psychiatry as a major new instrument of social
control.

Westphal's comment on the advisability of law reform was
part of a larger debate. In 1869, a new penal code for the
entire North German Confederation was to be enacted, Prussia's
code serving as a model. (An historical aside: homosexuality
was punishable in Prussia by burning at the stake up to 1794,
by imprisonment followed by lifelong banishment up to 1837, and
by imprisonment up to 1968--as part of the German Democratic
Republic. Ten draft revisions considered between 1794 and 1851
varied between imprisonment for various terms and no penalty at
all.)[12] The severity of Paragraph 143 was criticized by a number
of important voices, including the Royal Prussian Deputation for
Public Health. This body, which represented the elite of the
medical establishment, unanimously recommended that Paragraph
143 be dropped entirely.[13] The same sentiment was expressed by
the Minister of Justice, Leonhardt, who had engineered the repeal
of Hanover's anti-homosexual legislation in 1840. Ulrichs, the
Hanoverian who fled before the Prussian law to Bavaria, prepared
a brief on the question which he published in 1870 as *Araxes*.
This, his eleventh book, bore the subtitle "A Call for the Liberation of Uranians from Penal Law."

Another brief was written by Dr. Károly Mária Benkert (1824-
1882) and published as an open letter to Minister Leonhardt in

Homosexual Couple Being Burned

(Zurich, 1482)

1869.[14] Benkert, who published this work under the pseudonym
Kertbeny, was a Hungarian by birth who spent most of his life
in Germany and also lived for a time in France. Benkert was
acquainted with Ulrichs and familiar with the arguments for the
emancipation of homosexuals he had advanced over the years.
They reappeared in Benkert's brief with a shift in emphasis
which likely reflects his experience in France. Guided by
Enlightenment thinking, which held that offenses against religion and morality in private did not fall within the purview of
of criminal law, the revolutionary Constituent Assembly had enacted a penal code in 1791 which removed homosexuality from
the list of punishable offenses. This action was reaffirmed
in the Napoleonic Code, and the same philosophy produced the
Bavarian penal code of 1813. Benkert cited these codes in his
brief and argued that the modern constitutional state had a duty
to disengage itself from matters of private morality.[15] And most
notably, the word homosexuality (Homosexualität) first appeared
in Benkert's open letter.

The Minister of Health, Education, and Religion, Heinrich
von Mühler, chose to pass over these arguments for reform. It
has been suggested that his thinking was primarily influenced
by his wife, who was known as a religious fanatic; officially,
on the other hand, Mühler justified the maintenance of Paragraph
143 in the draft he presented to the Reichstag by citing "the
consciousness of right among the people"--an ominous anticipation

of the Nazi reliance upon the "healthy sensibility of the people"
as a legal norm.[16] The draft code was formally adopted by the
Reichstag in which Jean Baptiste von Schweitzer was seated.

Summarizing the developments of the 1860s, it is striking
that the four men discussed here--Schweitzer, Ulrichs, Westphal,
and Benkert--were lawyers and doctors. It is coincidental yet
paradigmatic that the first two, who come to our attention at
the beginning of the decade, were lawyers while the second pair,
who appeared in print in 1869, were both doctors. The trend of
the times was to take the issue out of the province of law and
to place it in the province of medicine, particularly psychiatry.
Had it not been for the reactionary Mühler, the homosexual emancipation movement of the succeeding decades might have developed
in an entirely different direction.

Nonetheless, this decade witnessed the end of homosexual
invisibility. One way in which this manifested itself was the
sudden proliferation of names for homosexuals. Under the impact
of the medieval injunction that homosexuality is a sin so horrible
that it should not even be mentioned among Christians,[17] the only
socially acceptable words up to the 1860s were *Sodomit*, *Päderast*,
and *Knabenschänder* (literally, "boy-ravisher").[18] Westphal's contrary (later, inverted) sexuality and Benkert's homosexuality
(later, homoeroticism) left heterosexuality as an unquestioned
norm precisely by not creating a new word for it. The creation
of new, more positive names has recurred as a major item on the

agenda of the homosexual emancipation movement from the time of
Ulrichs to contemporary gay (!) liberation. Of the early writers,
Ulrichs alone placed homosexuality in a new perspective by devis-
ing two categories: *Urning* and *Dioning* (a bisexual accordingly
was an *Uranodioning*). The two doctors both coined terms which
turned on the word sex; Ulrichs spoke of love *(mannmännliche
Liebe)*.

Another sign of the times was the escalating estimates of
the actual number of homosexuals. In *Vindex* (1864), Ulrichs
boldly suggested that Uranians might constitute as much as .002%
of the German population. Five years later, Westphal allowed
that homosexuality "occurs more frequently than is realized."
And in his open letter, Benkert stated stated that Berlin, with
700,000 inhabitants, had perhaps 10,000 homosexuals--1.4% of the
urban population. These estimates appear astonishingly low in
light of modern studies, but they nonetheless document the end
of homosexual invisibility.

The generation of the 1860s was the first to have fully
experienced Germany's modernization, which began with the establishment of the *Zollverein* (Tariff Union) in 1834 and the laying
of the first intercity railroad link in 1835. Industrialization
and urbanization developed quickly over the next thirty years,
and the appearance of homosexuality was one of many social consequences. As trade barriers between petty German principalities
fell, there was a striking change in the landscape: the walls

which had encircled the feudal trade centers were torn down,
and the open space which now ringed the inner city was often
planted and turned into a public park. A strikingly recurrent
feature of the medical and criminological literature of this
period is the apprehension of homosexuals in the newly created,
impersonal public space of parks (Schweitzer!) and train sta-
tions (Westphal's case studies!).[19]

Prior to the wave of urbanization, the vast majority of
German homosexuals lived in peasant villages where it was impossible for them to imagine themselves as a minority, to recognize
themselves as a group with shared interests. The eccentric
bachelor or spinster (and many homosexuals married in any case)
may have been the object of mild suspicion or concern to village
neighbors, but they would not automatically associate such forms
of deviance with the sin of Sodom. Only the educated aristocracy
and the rising urban *Bürgertum* had access to information about
other cultures in which homosexual relations were acceptable or
even celebrated.[20] Urban homosexuals developed the ritualized
forms of interaction which would facilitate mutual recognition,
and effeminate behavior on the part of males first became a
caste mark in the cities. These developments form the historical
context for Ulrichs' writings.

It is worth noting that Ulrichs' theory of homosexuality
was in large measure an *apologia pro vita sua*. He was apparently
very effeminate even as a boy, and it is unlikely that the concept

of *anima muliebris in corpore virili inclusa*--a female soul con-
fined in a male body--would have been formulated otherwise. In
Inclusa (1864; the title refers to the Latin formula), Ulrichs
said the following:

> Apart from the womanly direction of our sexual desire,
> we Uranians bear another womanly element within us which,
> it appears to me, offers proof positive that nature devel-
> oped the male germ within us physically but the female
> spiritually. We bear this other womanly element from our
> earliest childhood on. Our character, the way we feel,
> our entire temperament is not manly: it is decidedly wo-
> manly. This inner womanly element is outwardly recog-
> nizable by our outwardly apparent womanly nature. Our
> outward nature is manly only in so far as education, the
> constant milieu in which we grew up, the social position
> we were given artificially trained us in manly manners. (21)

Many homosexuals later active in the emancipation struggle, particularly its anti-feminist wing, bitterly attacked this formu-
lation and felt that it was an insult. This masculine protest
was itself, however, a damaging concession to the crude arguments of social Darwinism, which joined with sexology in the
creation of theories about homosexual degeneration *(Entartung)*:

> The more indistinct the physical and psychical sexual
> characters appear in the individual, the deeper it is
> below the present level of perfect homologous monosexu-
> ality obtained in the evolution of manifold thousands
> of years. (22)

It remains for a future social history to document the extent to
which sex roles have been transformed as a result of modernization.
One historian has persuasively argued that the *fin-de-siècle* cult
of androgyny was a form of "aesthetic opposition" or passive protest against bourgeois heterosexuality.[23] This much is clear:

Ulrichs sought to explain and justify a form of public miscon-
duct--male effeminacy--which was and is stigmatized by both
heterosexuals and homosexuals.[24]

NOTES

1. August Bebel, *Aus meinem Leben* (Berlin: Dietz, 1961),
p. 230.

2. Quoted in Richard Linsert, *Kabale und Liebe: Über Politik und Geschlechtsleben* (Berlin: Man, 1931), p. 178.

3. The letters are printed in the *Jahrbuch für sexuelle
Zwischenstufen* I (1899) 36-70.

4. John Addington Symonds, *A Problem in Modern Ethics*
London: n.p., 1896), p. 84.

5. *Vindex* (Leipzig: Max Spohr, 1898), p. 97.

6. Cited in Magnus Hirschfeld, *Die Homosexualität des
Mannes und des Weibes* (Berlin: Louis Marcus, 1914), p. 958.

7. More detailed summaries of Ulrichs' theories are to
be found in Chapter 7 of Symonds' *A Problem in Modern Ethics*
and in Hirschfeld, *op. cit.*, pp. 954-967.

8. Ulrichs' theory of bisexuality is presented in a novel
by Adolf Wilbrandt entitled *Fridolins heimliche Ehe* (1875).
Published in translation as *Fridolin's Mystical Marriage* in
1884, it was the first homoerotic novel to appear in the United
States. Cf. Noel I. Garde, *The Homosexual in Literature* (New
York: Village Press, 1959) p. 11; *Fridolin* belongs in Garde's
primary list.

9. Cited in Hirschfeld, *op. cit.*, p. 967.

10. In "Die conträre Sexualempfindung, Symptom eines neuro-
pathischen (psychopathischen) Zustandes," *Archiv für Psychiatrie
und Nervenkrankheiten* II (1869) 108.

11. Klaus Dörner, *Bürger und Irre: Zur Sozialgeschichte
und Wissenschaftssoziologie der Psychiatrie* (Frankfurt am Main:
Europäische Verlagsanstalt, 1969), p. 358.

12. Cf. Gisela Ingeborg Bleibtreu-Ehrenberg, *Sexuelle Abartigkeit im Urteil der abendländischen Religions-, Geistes- und Rechtsgeschichte im Zusammenhang mit der Gesellschaftsentwicklung* (Bonn: Ph.D. diss., 1970), pp. 369-433. Lesbians were affected by the law until 1851, when it was restricted to males.

13. The position paper of the Delegation appears as an appendix in Richard von Krafft-Ebing, *Der Conträrsexuale vor dem Strafrichter* (Leipzig and Vienna: Franz Deuticke, 1894), pp. 35-37.

14. *Paragraph 143 des preussischen Strafgesetzbuches vom 14.4.1851 und seine Aufrechterhaltung als Paragraph 152 im Entwurf eines Strafgesetzbuches für den Norddeutschen Bund. . . .* (Leipzig: Serbes, 1869); reprinted in *Jahrbuch* VII/1 (1905) 1-66.

15. For a more detailed summary of Benkert's position, see John Lauritsen and David Thorstad, *The Early Homosexual Rights Movement (1864-1935)* (New York: Times Change Press, 1974), pp. 6-8.

16. Hirschfeld, *op. cit.*, pp. 961, 963.

17. This occurs in German as early as 1620. Paragraph VI/5 of the *Landrecht des Herzogtums Preussen* treats "Alle Unkeuschheit so wider die Natur und sonst in was Weise auch immer es geschehen kann und für züchtige Ohren nicht zu erzählen gebühret."

18. Interestingly, Carl Ludwig Klose had remarked in 1837 that *Knabenschändung* was "far more appropriate" than the "euphemistic name of the ancients," namely *Päderastie*, in his article under that word in J. S. Ersch and J. G. Gruber's *Allgemeine Encyclopädie der Wissenschaften und Künste*, 3. Section, 9. Theil (Leipzig: F. A. Brockhaus, 1837), p. 147. Cf. also the entries under "Knabenliebe," "Knabenschänder," and "Sodomei" in Grimm's *Wörterbuch*.

19. Cf. Dörner, *op. cit.*, pp. 322-323.

20. A noteworthy exception was the Swiss milliner Heinrich Hössli, who lived in the village of Glarus. His two-volume *Eros: Die Männerliebe der Griechen. . . .* (Glarus: By the author, 1836; St. Gallen: Scheitlin, 1838) was an astonishing accomplishment for a self-tutored and totally isolated individual , but it remained without impact on the future homosexual emancipation movement. Cf. Ferdinand Karsch-Haack, *Der Putzmacher von Glarus Heinrich Hössli* (Leipzig: Max Spohr, 1903) for a detailed study.

21. *Inclusa* (Leipzig: Max Spohr, 1898), pp. 25-26.

19

22. Quoted in Elizabeth Fee, "Science and Homosexuality," *The Universities and the Gay Experience* (New York: Gay Academic Union, 1974), p. 37. Cf. also Vern L. Bullough, "Homosexuality and the Medical Model," *Journal of Homosexuality* I (1974) 99-110.

23. Gert Mattenklott, *Bilderdienst: Ästhetische Opposition bei Beardsley and George* (Munich: Rogner & Bernhard, 1970), pp. 45-57, 60-105. For other uses of androgyny, see A. J. L. Brust, "The Image of the Androgyne in the Nineteenth Century," *Romantic Mythologies,* ed. Ian Fletcher (London: Routledge & Kegan Paul, 1967), pp. 1-96.

24. On the homosexual stigmatization of effeminacy, see Martin Dannecker and Reimut Reiche, *Der gewöhnliche Homosexuelle* (Frankfurt am Main: Fischer, 1974), pp. 351-356.

CHAPTER II

THE EMERGENCE OF ORGANIZATIONS

1871 - 1918

During the eight-year period of Ulrichs' isolated struggle,
Germany was undergoing rapid changes in the economic and political spheres. German nationalism, which petty princes had barely
been able to contain for several decades, was moving toward ful-
fillment; and the rising class of industrial magnates, already
wealthier than their despotic rulers, were eager to see the fall
of the last barriers to a free market economy, the internal tar-
iffs and duties that were a remnant of feudalism. The Austro-
Prussian War, in which Bavaria sided with Austria, led in 1867
to the establishment of the North German Confederation.[1] Only
three years later, German victory in the Franco-Prussian War led
to the final integration of the South German kingdoms. The Second
Reich was proclaimed at Versailles in January, 1871, and Paragraph
152 of the North German penal code, Prussia's old Paragraph 143,
was adopted for the entire Reich as Paragraph 175.

German unification under Prussian leadership was an enormous
setback to Ulrichs, who now stood alone against the assembled
might of the Prussian bureaucracy in Berlin, the Catholic Church
(with its political arm, the Center Party), and a Reichstag faced

by more pressing concerns than penal reform. Ulrichs, who now
lived in Stuttgart, retreated from print until 1875, and his
next book was something entirely new--a collection of poems on
homoerotic themes entitled *Auf Bienchens Flügeln* (On the Wings
of a Bee). Ulrichs waited another five years to issue his final
polemic, a memorandum to the legislative bodies in Berlin and
Vienna entitled *Kritische Pfeile* (Critical Arrows). At the age
of fifty-five, physically and spiritually drained, Ulrichs aban-
doned the cause of homosexual emancipation. Like so many German
homosexuals before him--one thinks immediately of Winckelmann
and Platen--Ulrichs made the Italian journey, moving first to
Naples and then, in 1883, to Aquila, an isolated town in the
Abruzzi Mountains, where he lived his last years in poverty and
exile. (For anyone familiar with this subcultural tradition of
southern flight, a special resonance is added to Mann's *Der Tod
in Venedig*.) Ulrichs went on to publish a collection of homoerotic stories, *Matrosengeschichten* (Sailor Stories), in 1885
and a small collection of poetry to memorialize the death of
Ludwig II in 1886. Until his death in 1895, he also issued a
small literary journal in classical Latin entitled *Alaudae* (Larks).

Ulrichs was an all but forgotten man in Germany, but his
memory was preserved by the one visitor he received in Aquila:
John Addington Symonds (1840-1893). Symonds had happened upon
Ulrichs' writings and conceived the idea of writing a scholarly
polemic on homosexuality himself; the two corresponded through-

out 1891, and in October Symonds arrived in Aquila for a two-day visit.[2] Two months after the visit Symonds published *A Problem in Modern Ethics*, which contains a lengthy chapter on Ulrichs' works. Through Symonds' collaboration with Havelock Ellis on the book *Sexual Inversion* (1897), Ulrichs' ideas entered the literature of homosexual defense in England at the same time that they were being rediscovered in Germany.

Had he spent his last years in Germany, Ulrichs might well have found others willing to join with him in the struggle for homosexual emancipation. In 1896 the first homophile periodical appeared in Berlin under the editorship of Adolf Brand (1874-?). It was to run until 1929, appearing at various points as a weekly, a monthly, and an annual. Entitled *Der Eigene*, a marvelous word suggesting "self," "same" (sex), and "different" (rather like the French *le particulier*), this lavish journal bore the subtitle "A Periodical for Masculine Culture, Art, and Literature." In the same year, a small study of homosexuality entitled *Sappho und Sokrates* was published in Leipzig by the firm of Max Spohr (1850-1905). The author, who published this book under the pseudonym Theodor Ramien, was Dr. Magnus Hirschfeld (1868-1935). Hirschfeld, Spohr, and a ministerial official named Erich Oberg met in Hirschfeld's Berlin apartment on May 15, 1897, and founded the first homosexual emancipation organization, the *Wissenschaftlich-humanitäres Komitee* (Scientific-Humanitarian Committee).

Spohr moved quickly to reprint Ulrichs' works, and by

1899 his firm had published twenty-three books on homosexuality, including a few novels and a translation of Edward Carpenter's *Homogenic Love in a Free Society* (1894). 1899 also brought the publication of the first volume of the *Jahrbuch für sexuelle Zwischenstufen* (Yearbook for Intersexual Variants), a scholarly journal which appeared under Hirschfeld's editorship until 1923. Its articles ranged over legal, medical, historical, and anthropological aspects of homosexuality; it also contained reports on the Committee's activities, reviews of fictional and non-fictional publications, and complete annual bibliographies of relevant works. These bibliographies reveal that one decade after Ulrich's death, 320 publications on homosexuality rolled off the presses of Germany in a single year. Hirschfeld took up the struggle for homosexual emancipation as optimistically as had Ulrichs; in the preface to the first volume of the *Jahrbuch* he expressed his hope that Paragraph 175, "whose existence besmirches the escutcheon of German justice, will not be carried into the new century."[3]

Looking back at the genesis of the organized homosexual emancipation movement many years later, Hirschfeld placed it firmly in the context of several other movements for reform:

It is no coincidence that the *Wandervogel* movement and the first country boarding schools were founded during the same brief timespan when, quite independent of one another, a number of sexual reform movements took shape. We will mention only [a few]: the Society for Control of Venereal Disease, which dared to call an evil by name when it was almost considered worse to mention it than to have it; the movement for the protection of

LEADERS OF THE SCIENTIFIC-HUMANITARIAN COMMITTEE

Left to right: Georg Plock, Dr. Ernst Burchard, Dr. Magnus Hirschfeld, Baron von Teschenberg

> maternity, which took up the cause of unwed mothers and
> illegitimate children, regarded as social pariahs no
> less than those afflicted with venereal disease; the
> Scientific-Humanitarian Committee, which took up the
> struggle for the justification and defense of congeni-
> tal homosexuals against legal and social persecution. .
> . . And above all there appeared on the scene the
> pioneers, then called "radical," of women's emancipa-
> tion. The first large rally for women's suffrage took
> place in Berlin in 1894, much to the astonishment and
> consternation of all the bourgeois parties; this was
> followed by the first large "International Women's
> Congress on Tasks and Goals of Women" in 1896. . . .
> It was also characteristic for the trend of the times
> that all of the strivings for natural modes of living
> and health increased their spread among the people dur-
> ing the final decades of the nineteenth century. Thus
> the first lodge against alcohol, which was followed by
> many others, was founded in Berlin in 1896. . . . I
> myself was actively involved in all these movements
> after settling in Berlin. (4)

The homosexual emancipation movement was one of a large panoply

of efforts for reform which came to be known collectively as

the *Lebensreformbewegung* (Life Reform Movement). This social

phenomenon has yet to receive a systematic investigation, and

a brief excursus on the circumstances which led to its rise is

in order.

Following the establishment of the Second Reich, the popu-

lation of Germany's metropolitan centers--Berlin, Munich, Hamburg,

and the Ruhr region--more than doubled within a short space of

time, and abysmal social conditions were the result. Chronic

housing shortage, unemployment, alcoholism, venereal disease,

police terrorism, social unrest--these were the problems faced

by the new city dwellers. The cry "Back to the land!" was voiced

frequently, and anti-Semitism provided another escape valve for the tensions of urban life. With the growth of large cities, of course, came the development of a sizable homosexual sub-culture. The police of Berlin had a tradition of tolerance toward homosexuality which reached back to the eighteenth cen-tury, and by 1914, Berlin was home to some forty homosexual bars as well as one to two thousand male prostitutes (a police estimate).[5]

The clientele of both the bars and the prostitutes was drawn from the new urban middle class, whose standard of living had risen dramatically during the *Gründerjahre* (1871-73). The prostitutes themselves were largely working-class youths, seek-ing to supplment their earnings or simply out of work. This reflects the fact that the income of German workers had scarcely changed since the sixties, and the industrial workers' living conditions were actually far worse than those of their parents on the farm. It was the new middle class whose status and new-found affluence was most immediately threatened by the economic fluctuations during the Wilhelmine era.

As the optimism and patriotic fervor of the *Gründerjahre* faded, middle-class Germans were quickly brought up short by the squalor and viciousness of life all around them; but the govern-ment was firmly in the hands of the Junkers and industrialists, and the middle class lacked the leadership necessary to have any impact on national politics. At the same time, the middle class was afraid of sinking to the level of mere laborers and rejected socialism as internationalistic and a movement of the faceless masses. It also rejected capitalism as un-German (as a "Jewish" import from England) and cherished feelings of moral superiority toward the upper classes. Unwilling to choose either of these alternatives, the middle class hit upon reform as the only acceptable solution to the urgent social problems.

The 1890s saw the rise of such diverse tendencies as the *Frauenbewegung* (women's movement), *Wandervogelbewegung* (youth movement), *Naturheilbewegung* (natural health movement)--all cited by Hirschfeld--as well as other, somewhat eccentric trends, such as the *Schrebergartenbewegung* (home vegetable garden movement), *Ernährungsreform* (nutritional reform) and related *Rohkostdiät* (macrobiotic diet), and *Kleiderreform* (clothing reform) with the allied *Freikörperkultur* (nudity movement). The German middle class became a kind of ideological proving ground for a wide range of promises of salvation: numerous quasi-religious cults appeared, promoting monism, theosophy, anthroposophy, various Oriental religions, and meditation. The movements provided a wide array of leaders and programs for the amorphous and politically leaderless middle class. In essence, the German *Kleinbürgertum* was striving to bring about social changes which the French bourgeoisie had achieved a full century earlier; but because few of the reformers questioned the overall political and economic system of Germany, their efforts were aimed not at revolution but instead at a humane amelioration of the most urgent

2. Jahrgang   Nr. 23   1. Dezember 1913

Preis 30 Pfg.

THE CULT OF NUDITY

Upper left: The cover of the nudist journal *Kraft und Schönheit* (Strength and Beauty), 1902

Upper right: The cover of the youth group journal *Vortrupp* (Vanguard), 1913

Below: Title page and frontispiece of Friedländer's *Renaissance des Eros Uranios*, 1904

social conflicts. The leaders of these movements were usually
highly educated and often academics--the highest professional status to which the middle class could aspire.

The Scientific-Humanitarian Committee was founded by a physician, a publisher, and a civil servant.[6] Dr. Hirschfeld was chairman of the Committee and firmly controlled its activities from 1897
into the 1920s. Hirschfeld was talented primarily as a scientist;
his gifts as an organizer were clearly secondary, and his motto
was *Per scientiam ad justitiam* (justice through knowledge). His
academic titles and numerous publications--a complete bibliography
runs to almost 200 titles[7]--lent him an aura of respectability and
authority which were a prerequisite for his leadership. Yet his
writings were generally discredited and he himself was often criticized by the academic establishment for his activism; and due to
the anti-Semitism of the German middle class, the fact that he was
a Jew worked both to his disadvantage and the Committee's.

The Committee's goal was first and foremost legal reform, and
its first action was the preparation and circulation of a three-
page petition which outlined the scientific and humanitarian reasons
for amending Paragraph 175 so that homosexual acts would be punishable only in cases involving coercion, public annoyance, or adult-
minor relations. Signatures were gathered only among the opinion
makers of Wilhelmine Germany--prominent scientists, lawyers, educa-
tors, writers, highly placed civil servants, church functionaries,
and the like. The Committee won the support of August Bebel and

Karl Kautsky, the leaders of the Social Democratic Party; and a
number of highly placed homosexuals (including Alfred Krupp)
politely but firmly refused to sign. Within a matter of months
a petition with some 900 signatures was presented to the Reichstag.[8]

Parliamentary consideration of the petition was taken up
in January of 1898, and the Committee received a firm rebuff.
The only members of the Reichstag who supported the proposed
reform were Social Democrats, led by August Bebel.[9] With the
exception of a single National Liberal, the representatives of
other parties expressed astonishment and outrage at the petition. Hirschfeld, however, regarded it as a major success that
he was personally received by Secretary Nieberding, head of the
Reich Office of Justice, who gave him a few words of advice:

> The government's hands are tied until the public knows
> that your demands are a matter of ethics and not just
> some sexual or scientific whim. You must educate the
> public so that it will understand what's involved if
> the government does away with this paragraph. (10)

His faith in the benevolence of the government and the petition's
usefulness restored, Hirschfeld resumed gathering signatures.
By 1914, a list of more than 3000 doctors, 750 university profes-
sors, and thousands of other signatures had been added to the
petition.[11]

Following Nieberding's suggestion, the Committee also prepared a brochure entitled *Was soll das Volk vom dritten Geschlecht
wissen?* (What Should the People Know about the Third Sex?). The

first edition, printed in 1901 by Max Spohr, was criticized in the Social-Democratic *Die Neue Zeit* as woefully inadequate:

> . . .this brochure provides page after page of more or less
> well known names with more or less empty titles from the
> present day, along with hollow phrases such as, "We ex-
> pressly emphasize that we do not contest the demands of
> Christian morality, whose ideals everyone should strive
> to fulfill. . . ." Thus the issuing Scientific-Humani-
> tarian Committee makes a deep bow to the controlling Cen-
> ter Party and to bigotry in general. (12)

The brochure went through various revisions and by 1914 had been distributed in 50,000 copies. Other propaganda materials prepared by the Committee brought the pre-World-War-I total to 100,000.[13]

"By far the most significant event for homosexuals during the past year," Hirschfeld wrote in 1903, was the death of Alfred Krupp, Germany's "cannon king" and a close friend of Kaiser Wilhelm II.[14] The November 15, 1902 issue of *Vorwärts*, the Social Demo-cratic newspaper, reported that Krupp had recently been expelled from Capri by the Italian authorities because of his homosexual activities. One week after his exposure Krupp was dead, an appar-ent suicide. The revelations in *Vorwärts*, adjudged by other jour-nalists to be a contemptible maneuver to discredit both Krupp and the Kaiser, had been couched in language which simultaneously called for the revision of Paragraph 175 and described Krupp's sexual activities as bourgeois decadence:

> The case must now be discussed in public with due regard
> to seriousness. . .because it offers a picture of capital-
> ist culture in the most garish colors. . . . The horrible
> picture of capitalist influence is not especially toned
> down by our discovery that this is a man of perverse
> orientation. The pity due the victim of a fateful error
> of nature must be denied when millions have been placed
> at the service of that sickness' gratification. (15)

The denunciation of Krupp was a source of no little embarrassment to the Committee, which refused to take a stand on the allegations. Opinion was divided as to whether such revelations, which "directed the attention of the broadest circles of the public to the homosexual question,"[16] served to advance the cause of legal reform or instead hindered it. But the Committee reached a position:

> It should be emphasized once again that indiscretions on the part of the Committee are not to be feared. The frequently suggested "path over corpses" will not be taken by us under any circumstances. (17)

The path over corpses—denunciations of homosexuals of high standing—was rejected in favor of a major statistical survey.

The Committee distributed 6611 questionnaires to Berlin students and factory workers in 1903, and the results were published in the *Jahrbuch* the following year: 2.2% of the population was homosexual, 1,200,000 Germans in all. Hirschfeld noted:

> These high figures will surely astonish many people, and I admit that I myself would have been surprised by them eight years ago, when the suicide of one of my patients led me to turn to the study of intersexual variants. Today I am acquainted with the lives and activities of many hundreds of homosexuals, and the figures no longer surprise me. I have observed all too often the skill, zeal, and success with which homosexuals manage to conceal their orientation even from those closest to them, their relatives and friends. (18)

The 1903 escalation of the homosexual percentage of the population —one thinks of the .002% estimate put forward in 1864 by Ulrichs and the 1.4% boldly suggested by Benkert in 1869—was well-suited to buttress the argument that Paragraph 175 was unjust because it was selectively enforced and moreover exposed large numbers of homosexuals to blackmail.

BERLIN CENSUS, MODERN STYLE

The Census-Taker: "How many children?"
The Mother: "Two daughters, one boy, one Uranian, and three
    homosexual intermediates."
(This cartoon appeared in the Munich cultural weekly *Jugend*
in 1905.)

Precisely this position was taken by Adolf Thiele in the
1905 Reichstag debate on reform of Paragraph 175--the only major
debate on the subject during the Wilhelmine era. The Committee's
petition, which now had some 5000 signatures, was again brought
before the Reichstag. Thiele argued: "For my part, I wouldn't
even admit that this is something sick; it's simply a deviation
from the usual pattern nature produces."[19] A right-wing Social
Democrat, Thiele was put in the unpleasant position of crossing
swords with a fellow party member, von Vollmar, who argued:

> . . .my colleague Thiele, as every other colleague who
> speaks on this matter, is taking a purely personal stand
> on the issue, and the Social Democracy has as little to
> do with this issue as any other party. (Quite right! on
> the Left. Hear! hear! on the Right.) (20)

With the sole exception of August Bebel, the left Social Democrats maintained silence on the issue of homosexuality. Reichstag opposition to penal reform was led by the Center Party, and
only a few members of any party other than the Social Democracy
voted in its favor.

Perhaps as a result of the failure of penal reform in the
Reichstag, the Committee began to revise its views on the tactic
of denunciation. In late 1905, it entertained an internal debate
on the merits of a massive self-denunciation: 1000 homosexuals
were to turn themselves in to the police and to insist that
charges be pressed.[21] The grandiose plan proved impracticable,
but Adolf Brand, the editor of *Der Eigene*, struck out on his own
course of action. He published a small brochure entitled *Kaplan*

NEW PRUSSIAN COAT OF ARMS

(The figure on the left is Wilhelm II, on the right--identified
by his embroidered handkerchief--Philipp zu Eulenburg. The scroll
at the bottom reads: "My sweetie, my little snookums, my one and
only cuddly bear." From *Jugend*, 1907.)

Dasbach und die Freundesliebe (Chaplain Dasbach and Comrade Love) in which Dasbach, leader of the Center Party, was exposed as the blackmail victim of a male prostitute. The tactic was regarded as a great success by the movement.

Such was not the case with the next denunciation, which was carried out by the highly respected editor of the socialist weekly *Die Zukunft*, Maximilian Harden. On November 17, 1906, Harden published a lead article entitled "Praeludium" which attacked a group of alleged homosexuals who were friends and close advisors of the Kaiser. The following week he published a second lead article, "Dies irae," in which Prince Philipp zu Eulenburg and Count Kuno von Moltke (adjutant to the Kaiser and mayor of Berlin) were directly accused of "secret immorality and unnatural vices."[22] Unlike the *Vorwärts* revelations concerning the Krupp case, in which the editors had at least said that they were interested in revision of Paragraph 175, Harden denounced these aristocrats under the pretense of national security; but he, too, was actually interested in weakening the Kaiser. Quite coincidentally yet another aristocrat, Prince Friedrich Heinrich of Prussia, was brought to court on charges of homosexuality.

German newspapers were suddenly full of the story, and it dominated their headlines for months: an anti-homosexual witch-hunt of unparalleled proportions was unleashed. Nearly every high government official and military officer was suspected or accused of homosexuality. Encouraged by Harden's success in bringing such charges before the public, Brand again came forward with a denunciation entitled *Fürst Bülow und die Abschaffung des Paragraph 175* (Prince Bülow and the Repeal of Paragraph 175), in which Bernhard von Bülow, Chancellor of Germany, was accused of homosexuality. A series of trials and hearings ensued which dragged on until June of 1909 and never resolved all the questions that were raised. Libel charges were pressed against Harden by Moltke and against Brand by Bülow. Eulenburg, who protested his innocence before the Reichstag, was charged with perjury.

The Committee's years of effort to change public opinion were quickly undone. In an amazing tactical blunder, especially in light of the Committee's resolve not to take the "path over corpses," Hirschfeld allowed himself to be called into court to give expert testimony as to the sexual orientation of Moltke. Hirschfeld gave his objective diagnosis: Moltke was homosexual. Hirschfeld's appearance in court and his readiness to make such a damaging statement outraged and terrified many of the financial sponsors of the Committee, who were (perhaps justifiably) afraid that he might someday give testimony against them.

Instead of pulling together when confronted with a crisis, the membership of the Committee began to melt away. Financial support from upper-class, pro-monarchist homosexuals decreased; total contributions to the Committee dropped from 17,115 Marks in 1907 to 6038 Marks in 1909. It would be years before the Committee regained the strength it had enjoyed before the

PANIC IN WEIMAR

"Wolfgang, let go of my hand! Here comes Magnus Hirschfeld!"
(This cartoon, from a 1907 issue of *Jugend*, shows a well-known
statue in Weimar of Germany's classic poets, Johann Wolfgang von
Goethe and Friedrich Schiller.)

scandal. As Hirschfeld noted somewhat blindly in the *Jahrbuch*, it was "just as in the myth of the ancient: a massive boulder slowly pushed up a hill plunged back down again."[23] Now busy making the rounds from one courtroom to another, Hirschfeld did not seem to grasp that he was doing anything wrong--after all, from knowledge to justice.

The wave of anti-homosexual sentiment stirred up by the scandals along with reaction against the women's emancipation movement led in late 1909 to the introduction of a draft penal code which ignored previous reform efforts and even extended Paragraph 175 to homosexual acts between women. It was scornfully noted by anti-feminists that this measure would advance equality of the sexes.[24] Although there had been some discussion in earlier years of the presence of lesbians in the women's movement,[25] the draft penal code appears to have evoked surprisingly little controversy. In 1904, Anna Rüling had addressed a meeting of the Scientific-Humanitarian Committee on the common interests of the women's and homosexual emancipation movements. She charged feminist organizations with "not lifting a finger. . .doing nothing, *absolutely nothing*"[26] to advance the cause of homosexual rights or to decrease the continued invisibility of lesbians. This was also the case in 1909.

One of the more conservative organizations within the women's movement was the League for the Protection of Maternity and Sexual Reform *(Bund für Mutterschutz und Sexualreform)*, which had been

Helene Stöcker

been founded in 1905 by Dr. Helene Stöcker (1869-1943), later

a director of the Scientific-Humanitarian Committee.[27] On Febru-

ary 10, 1911, the League held a meeting at which Hirschfeld and

Stöcker spoke on homosexuality and the Committee's petition cam-

paign. The League adopted a resolution which may well stand as

the first statement by any women's group on homosexuality. It

termed the proposal to criminalize lesbianism "a grave error"[28]

and continued:

> It would not remove inequality [of the sexes] but double
> injustice. The door would be thrown open to informers
> and blackmailers, and unmarried working women who live
> together would be shamefully harassed without protecting
> any legal interests. As a minimum, this gathering re-
> gards it as absolutely necessary that medical experts
> --especially sexologists and psychiatrists--as well as
> women be included in the deliberations on this question. (29)

The basic principle underlying this resolution was expressed by

Stöcker one month later in the pages of *Die neue Generation* (The

New Generation), a journal which she edited:

> Our modern state is built upon the concept of individual
> freedom. Backward absolutism and intolerance still rule
> in the realm of sexual morality; worse yet, sexual moral-
> ity is placed under the law. We cannot truly speak of a
> libertarian state or a country of culture until, along-
> side legal and social freedom of religion, we have
> achieved individual freedom in the most private part of
> private life--love life. If religion is a private matter,
> love life is no less! (30)

The ties between the Scientific-Humanitarian and the women's move-

ment stood in stark contrast to the anti-feminism of the second

homosexual emancipation organization of the Wilhelmine era: the

Community of the Special *(Gemeinschaft der Eigenen)*.

The Community was founded by Adolf Brand, Wilhelm Jansen, and Benedict Friedländer on May 1, 1902, and its members were drawn largely from the readership of *Der Eigene*. Its leading theorist was Friedländer (1866-1908), a wealthy private scholar. In his *Renaissance des Eros Uranios* (Renaissance of Eros Uranios, 1904), he set down the goals of his movement in terms that partly paralleled Stöcker's view:

> The negative side of our libertarian goal is therefore clear and simple enough: it consists merely of carrying over legal and social freedom from religion to the area of private love life. We have come far enough that the agreement of all parties on this point should soon be achieved. (31)

On this point there was certainly no disagreement between Friedländer's Community and Hirschfeld's Committee. Friedländer, however, continued:

> The positive goal. . .is the revival of Hellenic chivalry (with the greatest possible avoidance of sexual excess) and its recognition by society. By chivalric love we mean in particular close friendship between youths and even more particularly the bonds between men of unequal ages. (32)

The Community looked to ancient Greece and Renaissance Italy as model civilizations and argued that Christian asceticism was responsible for the demise of homosexual relations. Friedländer, who was married, advocated pedophile relations combined with family life, and Brand contrasted his journal with Hirschfeld's *Jahrbuch* by saying that he wanted to show "more the Hellenic side of things."[33] Politically, *Der Eigene* had at first a Stirnerian anarchist editorial stance which evolved over time to an anti-Marxist "libertarian socialism" or "socialitarianism," closely reflecting Friedländer's admiration of Eugen Dühring.[34]

Just as the Scientific-Humanitarian Committee emerged from
the broader sexual reform movement at the turn of the century, the
Community of the Special was indebted to the nudity cult which was
part of the *Lebensreformbewegung* (see Figure 4). Friedländer was
a member of a nudist organization as early as 1893 and later con-
tributed to some of its periodicals; he described its impact in
this way:

> Of all the modern movements which were started for another
> purpose but which, as a side effect, redound to the bene-
> fit of Eros, the one which must be named in the very first
> place is the revival of naked athletics following the
> Hellenic model. (35)

The advocates of nudity attacked prevailing sex norms in a contra-
dictory way, directly challenging the taboo on nakedness but simultaneously asserting that--a healthy mind in a healthy body--they
were interested not in sex but in hygiene. Friedländer's views
on pedophile relations reproduced this contradiction by asseverating
that relations with youths were to be erotic but not sexual. Homosexual relations, he felt, were unnatural, whereas:

> As soon as *natural* people (who are unclothed people) in a
> *natural* mood (which is unconstrained happiness) deal with
> each other in a *natural* way (which is harmless friendliness),
> Eros will surely be roused. (36)

Many of the ideological features of the Community of the Special
can perhaps best be explained in terms of the fact that by advocating
pedophile relations, two taboos were being broken simultaneously:
the Judeo-Christian taboo on same-sex relations and the Germanic
taboo on sexual relations between persons of different ages (itself a manifestation of the incest taboo). It must have appeared

Benedict Friedländer

to members of the Community that their sexual orientation was
totally irreconcilable with modern society, which in turn led
such men as Brand, Erich Mühsam (1878-1934),[37] and John Henry
Mackay (1864-1933)[38] to advocate anarchism.

Friedländer asserted that a "new phase of the emancipation
movement"[39] had begun with the publication in 1900 of *Liebling-
minne und Freundesliebe in der Weltlitteratur* (Chivalric Affec-
tion and Comrade Love in World Literature), an anthology of homoerotic literature from Greek to modern times edited by Élisàr von
Kupffer. In an "ethical-political introduction" to this book,
Kupffer sharply attacked the Scientific-Humanitarian Committee:

> . . .I must take a stand against the entire recent direc-
> tion and attack the sickly craze of our pseudo-scientific
> age for principles. It has now become fashionable in
> humane-scientific and related circles to talk about a
> "third" sex whose soul and body are supposedly mismatched.
> . . . This word "Urning". . .[or] "Uranian" has spread
> like a menacing epidemic. The matter has been investi-
> gated, criticized, categorized, medico-hypnotized, popu-
> larized, and God knows what all. It has finally attracted
> people who. . .intended [only] to feather their nest. . . .
> And the most vexing thing about all this is that in the
> process, the elite of our entire human history has been
> so deformed that these brilliant thinkers and heroes are
> scarcely recognizable in their Uranian petticoats. (47)

As bisexuals, Friedländer and other members of the Community knew
from their own experience that a homosexual response was not limited
to a minority of congenital inverts. For the Community, however,
heterosexual relations were relegated to purely procreative ends
and the aesthetic superiority of pedophile relations was asserted.

Those with an exclusively hetero- or homosexual orientation
were ridiculed by Friedländer as *Kümmerlinge* (atrophied or puny

beings); he was also excited by the bizarre hypotheses of Dr.

Gustav Jaeger, who asserted that sexual attraction was based on

sense of smell and that supervirile individuals exuded an aroma

which charmed both men and women.[41] Friedländer and Kupffer ex-

hibited all the anti-scientific resentment of the German middle

class confronted by technological modernization:

> Just what is the science of the Scientific-Humanitarian
> Committee?
> With minor variations and insignificant additions, the
> content of the twelve brochures by the jurist K. H. Ulrichs
> has been spread among the people, not just by Mr. Hirsch-
> feld but also by the entire medical establishment. Ulrichs
> was an honest, courageous, and original man. His truly
> pioneering steps had correspondingly little success at
> the time. The officious doctors with their armor of
> authority arrived a generation later, when the question
> was no longer so unmentionable. They thought they had
> scented out a new area for theory and practice--and
> their sense of smell [!] did not let them down. Ulrichs
> was shouted down at the Munich Jurists Congress in 1867,
> and he died a lonely man at Aquila in the Abruzzi Moun-
> tains in 1895. His medical imitators, each in his own
> way, enjoyed tolerable successes in money, respect, or
> both. The one was satisfied with commercial speculation
> on the sexual excitability of the reading public, which
> bought up numerous printings of his so-called *Psycho-
> pathia sexualis*; others made their way with hypnotism
> and, for a fee, suggested away the love of a friend and
> replaced it with love for a woman; yet others carried
> out successful business via agitation. (42)

Friedländer himself maintained a double membership in the Committee

and the Community until 1906, when he led a secession from the

Committee, charging Hirschfeld with financial and administrative

mismanagement.

The membership of the Community realized that the Committee's

petition, which called for the legalization of same-sex relations

only between those over the age of sixteen, neglected their interests.

They were also affronted by Hirschfeld's personal effeminacy and his sweeping classification of all homosexuals in one category. Perhaps their most cogent argument against the Committee, however, was this:

> Taken by itself, the very fact that the general public never sees anyone but doctors in the movement's leadership must further the erroneous notion that the movement is concerned with disease or at least some kind of sickness. Certainly sickness can be pitied, the sick can be treated "humanely," and a "cure" can even be attempted; but equality will never be accorded to those who are held to be physically inferior.
> The more progressive doctors have now expressly dropped the dogma that same-sex love is a sickness; they had to, of course, or their clients would have left them. (43)

Friedländer charged Hirschfeld with opportunism in refusing to acknowledge the existence of bisexuality and insisting upon the existence of a third sex. Hirschfeld in turn accused Friedländer of proving "grist for the mill of our enemies"[44] by propounding the superiority of homosexual relations with a bisexual context. The third-sex theory was under sharp and cogent attack from Friedländer, Freud, and others, and Hirschfeld quietly put it aside in about 1910.

The views of the Community of the Special were strikingly similar to those of the *Georgekreis*, the elite circle of writers associated with the poet Stefan George (1868-1933). Although George's homoerotic verse cannot be treated within the confines of this book, two brief pronouncements from the circle are worth reproducing here. Friedrich Gundolf and Friedrich Wolters, the editors of the Georgean *Jahrbuch für die geistige Bewegung*

(Yearbook for the Spiritual Movement), wrote an attack on Hirschfeld and the mass culture of America in terms that paralleled
Friedländer's. Erotic relations between men, they said, have
nothing

> . . .to do with a medieval, witch-hunting section of the
> law or a ridiculous medical classification scheme. Rather
> we have always believed that something essentially forma-
> tive for German culture as a whole is to be found in these
> relations. . . . It is not moral prejudice which leads
> people to be shocked by this type of friendship: . . . .
> it is the antipathy of unfeeling, essentially American
> people for any form of heroized love. It should be
> apparent that we have nothing to do with those far from
> charming people who whimper for the repeal of certain
> laws, for the most revolting attacks against us have
> issued from precisely those circles. (45)

In his *Norm Entartung Verfall* (Ideal - Degeneration - Ruin), Kurt
Hildebrandt, another "disciple" of the "master," asserted that
Greek pederasty had led to "an enhancement of masculinity"; he con-
tinued:

> It is incomprehensible that these forms should be confused
> with that type of homosexuality about which such a ruckus
> is made today. The latter arises contrarily in groups of
> effeminate men; it counteracts military and intellectual
> manliness; it tends toward the sexual, not the erotic.
> This modern abuse can be suspected of degeneration and
> is certain of ruin. (46)

There is a certain poignancy to the fact that these words were
published shortly after Hitler came to power. Whether or not
they were "effeminate," German homosexuals by the hundreds of
thousands were soon to be interned in concentration camps. George
himself emigrated to Switzerland shortly before Hitler came to
power, offended by one aspect of Nazism: the fact that it was a
mass movement.

Gundolf and Wolters advocated Catholicism as a weapon for fighting capitalism (which for them was synonymous with modernization), and this points to another feature of the Community of the Special. Some of its members, notably Élisàr von Kupffer and Eduard von Mayer, did not share Friedländer's vehement anti-clericalism.[47] They were interested instead in a revival of classical Greek, medieval Christian, and humanistic Renaissance values, much along the lines of the contemporaneous neo-Romantic movement in English homophile circles.[48] The figure opposite illustrates the cultural ideals of this wing of the Community. The photograph, presumably taken in Florence, shows a youth with a lute seated in a *sgabello* chair of the type popular in English pre-Raphaelite and German Nazarene circles in the nineteenth century. A number of unidentifiable works of art adorn the chamber: the statue is similar to the Praxitelean Apollo, and the three small paintings are of St. John the Baptist, St. Sebastian, and Jesus (bearing the cross)--all martyrs for their love. These Mediterranean elements are placed within a characteristically Northern ensemble, evoking seventeenth-century Flemish and Dutch interior painting; recent scholarship on Dutch painting has come to interpret the playing of a musical instrument before framed objects as a metaphor for eroticism. Although there may be a precise emblematic meaning to the arrangement, the eclectic assemblage of evocative objects works more by connotation than denotation to create an atmosphere of elevated and aristocratic aestheticism.

Renaissance Idyll

Aestheticism was the major program of Adolf Brand's *Der Eigene*, the journal of "masculine culture, art, and literature," but his hopes for a radical yet cultural homosexual movement were never fulfilled. The Community of the Special never approached the fame or influence of the Scientific-Humanitarian Committee. Friedländer's attempt to establish a Secession was cut short by his death in 1908, and Brand served a jail sentence in the same year as a result of the libel suit brought by Chancellor Bülow—Brand's one moment of glorious notoriety. Although *Der Eigene* continued to appear until 1929, perhaps the greatest impact upon larger events was made by Wilhelm Jansen (1866-1943), a co-founder of both the Community and the *Jungwandervogel*.

The man who followed most closely in Friedländer's footsteps was Hans Blüher (1888-1952). Blüher was something of a lone wolf: he never joined the Community, and his anti-Semitism quickly put him at odds with Hirschfeld. But Blüher managed to created a tremendous sensation with the publication of a single, best-selling book, *Die deutsche Wandervogelbewegung als erotisches Phänomen* (The German *Wandervogel* Movement as an Erotic Phenomenon, 1912). Through an ingeniously syncretic approach to the writings of Freud, Plato, Nietzsche, and Friedländer, Blüher devised a compelling analysis of the youth movement as a product of homoerotic attraction between men and boys. In a book published in 1917, *Die Rolle der Erotik in der männlichen Gesellschaft* (The Role of Eroticism in Male Society), Blüher systematized his theories into an elaborate

Hans Blüher

defense of bisexuality. Echoing Friedländer, Blüher argued that
the family was the institutionalization of heterosexual desires
while the political state arose from equally natural male homosexual relations. The true *typus inversus*, as distinct from the
effeminate homosexual, was seen as the founder of patriarchal
society and ranked above the heterosexual in terms of his capacity
for leadership and heroism.

The history of the German youth movement need not be spelled
out in any detail here, as it has already been dealt with in two
English-language treatments.[49] In outline, the movement began in
the late 1890s, reached its highpoint around World War I, and then
subsided into a sizable but noncontroversial stasis; the various
youth organizations of the 1920s were later to be subsumed into
Hitler Youth. In many respects, the youth movement enjoyed a renaissance in the hippie movement of the 1960s: both arose in protest against the school system, middle-class family life, and the
crass materialism of technological, urban culture. Both promised
a total renewal of society through a return to nature and trans-
cendental values, and both foundered on this ambivalence between
protest and escapism.

More attention must, however, be given to that part of the
youth movement's history which linked it with homosexuality. The
Wandervogel (literally, "migratory bird") movement started in 1896
as a small group of Berlin school boys given to camping trips,
treks through the country in colorful, traditional clothes, the

strict avoidance of women, and occasional smoking, drinking,

and sex. By 1906, the *Wandervogel* had spread over Northern Ger-

many, and in 1907, a Southern branch began operations with a

somewhat different orientation: separate but equal women's groups

were encouraged, abstinence from tobacco, alcohol, and sex was

demanded, and the groups were placed under the close supervision

of a council of parents and teachers.

When the anti-homosexual hysteria resulting from the Eulen-

burg scandal reached its peak in 1908 and 1909, several leaders

of the movement, notably Wilhelm Jansen, were forced to resign.

Jansen and his following formed the core of a counter-organiza-

tion which constituted itself in 1910 as the *Jungwandervogel*

(Young *Wandervogel*). The *Jungwandervogel*, which numbered around

1500, rightly pointed out that the original spirit and program of

the movement was being eroded by a leadership increasingly in the

hands of puritanical adults; the clothed males in Figure 4 illus-

trate this trend within the movement. But as far as homosexual-

ity was concerned, the *Jungwandervogel* never really put its cards

on the table. Instead, it issued ambiguous pronouncements like this

one, from the first issue of its official journal:

Now no one can deny that the need for friendship is at its
strongest between the ages of twelve and twenty. Generally,
the boy from a middle-class background cannot find at home
the kind of relaxed, intimate involvement which he rightly
demands. And that teachers at public schools become friends,
true friends with their pupils—this appears only in school
journals or eulogies for deceased pedagogues. But precisely
this: friendly relations with an older person, who doesn't
simply patronize a boy because of his inexperience. . .this is

> what made the *Wandervogel* great. Our binding force is
> not the will to comradeship but rather the will to
> friendship. (50)

The emphasis on friendship in this statement gives it an unmistakable homosexual ring, particularly when one considers the nuances of the word in German (homosexual "lovers" are called "friends"). But in contrast to the forthright declarations of the homosexual emancipation movement, the declarations of the *Jungwandervogel* were far from transparent.

And so it remained for the gadfly Blüher to reveal in *Die deutsche Wandervogelbewegung als erotisches Phänomen* that neither comradeship nor even friendship but outright homoeroticism was the binding force of the *Jungwandervogel* and that the founders and original leaders of the early movement had all been homosexual. The publication of Blüher's treatise was quickly followed by denials from within the movement and by charges from without that it was a front for a club of pederasts. The *Jungwandervogel* found itself in an increasingly isolated position within the movement, which in any case was now further factionalizing over questions of lifestyle and rapidly moving to the right in basic political orientation.

Largely due to the influence of Gustav Wyneken (1875-1964), the *Jungwandervogel* steered clear of the nationalistic, racist course taken by the youth movement as a whole. A pacifist and a socialist, Wyneken was one of Germany's most renowned innovators in the field of education. After World War I, he briefly held a high

post in the Ministry of Education; but his pedagogic efforts
were largely limited to heading the Free School Community at
Wickersdorf, which he founded in 1906 and led until it was closed
by the Nazis.

In his book *Eros* (1921), Wyneken advocated "heroic asceticism"
in sexual matters; but his entire educational theory was based
upon an erotic relationship between teacher and pupil. Wyneken's
recognition of the value of adolescence as a unique stage of human
existence and not just an immature phase on the way to adulthood
led him to advocate an autonomous *Jugendkultur* (youth culture),
an idea with striking affinities to the counter-culture program
of the 1960s. And just as hippies formed the vanguard of the
counter-culture, Wyneken saw the *Wandervogel* as opening a breach
in bourgeois society which could be broadened into *Jugendkultur*.
As a homosexual, Wyneken was closely affiliated with the *Jungwandervogel*; and he was alarmed at the factionalization and the
growing power of authoritarian leaders within the movement as a
whole.

Wyneken and Jansen mobilized one final effort to salvage the
original spirit and unity of the movement: in 1913, all the various
splinter groups created an umbrella organization, Free German
Youth *(Freideutsche Jugend)*. Most of the factions within the
movement, which now numbered about 40,000, had private doubts
about the ultimate success of Free German Youth, but they all
sent representatives to the organization's first national con-

gress, which was held in October, 1913, on a mountain peak in central Germany called the *Hohe Meissner*. The two to three thousand people present were swept away by Wyneken's oratory. The groups managed temporarily to paper over their differences in a statement (authored by Wyneken) which became known as the Meissner Creed:

> Free German Youth, on their own initiative, under their own responsibility, and with deep sincerity, are determined to shape their own lives independently. For the sake of this inner freedom they will under any and all circumstances take united action. (51)

The grandiose verbiage of the Creed cannot conceal its lack of any real content, and within a year the groups so tentatively united were finally completely sundered by the onset of World War I. The right-wing majority of Free German Youth jubilantly marched off to war, singing the old *Wandervogel* songs to which new, chauvinistic verses were added. The pacifist stance adopted by *Jungwandervogel* adherents was pointless in the face of universal conscription.

This rather lengthy excursus on the youth movement has served to point up some important trends in the pre-war period. The developments within the youth movement as well as the women's movement indicate that homosexuality had become a significant issue beyond the confines of the homosexual emancipation movement itself. Another trend which was to have an enormous impact on the entire nation was the growing polarization within politics, sexual and otherwise. The youth movement split irreconcilably over the issue

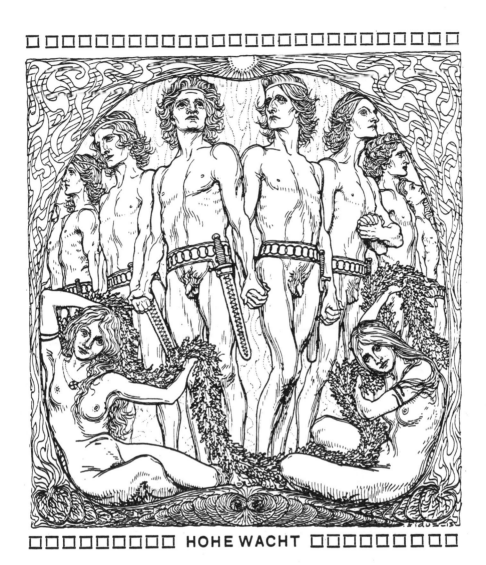

HIGH VIGIL

(This drawing by Fidus was the frontispiece of the first Free German
Youth publication, issued shortly after the Hohe Meissner meeting.)

of the sexual rights of youth: strict chastity was demanded by
those within the movement who espoused anti-Semitic, nationalistic, and authoritarian policies, while the *Jungwandervogel*
combined eroticism (however vaguely defined) with socialism and
pacifism.

Within the homosexual emancipation movement there was a deep
factionalization between the Committee and the Community: Brand
described himself as "the most decided opponent" of Hirschfeld and
spoke of the "fundamental difference in our methods of struggle."[52]
The point has already been made that the Committee was an organization of men and women, whereas the Community was exclusively
male. The Committee, which by 1914 had more than 1000 members,
was motivated by political goals; the Community (exact membership
unknown, but perhaps in the hundreds) saw itself as political
only in a negative sense, as cultural in a positive sense. Thus
the Committee was open to outside groups--the feminist movement,
national political parties, and indeed the general public--while
the Community was a closed group, aiming to create precisely the
feeling of cohesive community which Germany irretrievably lost in
the process of modernization.

Further, the Committee was rapidly becoming an international
organization: beyond its chapters in Berlin, Leipzig, Munich, and
Frankfurt, it set up branches in Amsterdam in 1911, London in 1912,
and Vienna in 1914. The Community, by contrast, was a local or
at most a national organization by virtue of the simple facts

that its only office was in Berlin and its publications were in
German. The Committee called homosexuals a third sex in an effort
to win the basic rights accorded the other two; the Community
scorned this as a beggarly plea for mercy and touted the notions
of supervirile bisexuality and the superiority of homosexuals over
heterosexuals in matters of taste and refinement.

The Committee based its efforts for legal reform on scientific
research in a number of disciplines; the Community propagated a
self-vindicating vision of Greek culture which blithely ignored
its social and political realities. Thus the Committee maintained
a non-partisan stance, relying heavily on the humanitarianism of
classical liberalism, while the Community enthused for an anarchistic utopia which would put women firmly in their place as child-
bearers and domestic servants and usher in a new era of male comradeship.

World War I brought the efforts of the homosexual emancipation movement to an almost complete halt. Although the Scientific-
Humanitarian Committee continued to hold meetings, half of its
members were called into military service.[53] The battlefield
deaths of many of these members were recorded in the *Jahrbuch,*
which also carried a long series of articles on the role of women
during the war. The Committee, taking a patriotic stand, broke
off its connection with foreign members who were citizens of enemy
states. Public forums and lectures were completely discontinued,
but the Committee set up a special fund to keep its basic functions

in operation--a move which was later sharply criticized by the

Nazis.[54] Early in 1915, Hirschfeld wrote:

> We must be, of course, and are prepared for any eventual-
> ity. What is necessary, however, is that the Committee
> be able to hold out and be there when--after what is
> hoped will be a quick, victorious end to the war--domestic
> reform efforts take up their activities and when the
> struggle for homosexual liberation picks up again, too. (55)

NOTES

1. Had Ludwig II invested in arms instead of art, the outcome
of this war might have been quite different. Coincidentally, the
same Congress of German Jurists which shouted down Ulrichs passed
a resolution wishing Ludwig, a homosexual, the happiness of a speedy
marriage. Cf. Magnus Hirschfeld, *Die Homosexualität des Mannes
und des Weibes* (Berlin: Louis Marcus, 1914), p. 958.

2. John Addington Symonds, *Letters*, vol. 3, ed. M. H. Schuel-
ler and R. L. Peters (Detroit: Wayne State University Press, 1969),
pp. 619, 650.

3. *Jahrbuch für sexuelle Zwischenstufen* I (1899) 3. The *Jahrbuch* will hereafter be cited as *JfsZ*.

4. Hirschfeld, *Geschlechtskunde*, vol. 1 (Stuttgart: Julius
Püttmann, 1926), p. 377.

5. The figures are from Abraham Flexner, *Prostitution in
Europe* (New York: The Century Co., 1914), pp. 31-32. Cf. also
Hirschfeld, *Berlins drittes Geschlecht* (Berlin: Hermann Seemann,
1905) and Hans Ostwald, *Männliche Prostitution* (Leipzig: Walther
Fiedler, 1906). Two sympathetic and closely observed fictional
treatments are Sagitta (i.e., John Henry Mackay), *Der Puppenjunge:
Die Geschichte einer namenlosen Liebe aus der Friedrichstrasse*
(Holland: By the author, 1926) and Hanns Heinz Ewers, *Armer Junge!
und acht andere Freundschafts-Novellen* (Berlin-Wilhelmshagen: Adolf
Brand, 1927).

6. In one account of the founding of the Committee (*JfsZ* XXIII
(1923) 183), Dr. Arthur Weil pointed to a fourth founder: Leopold
von Meerescheidt-Hüllesem, who was head of the section of Berlin
police for homosexual matters (a division with some ten employees!).
It appears that when Meerescheidt-Hüllesem died in 1900, he left
to Hirschfeld a list of twenty to thirty thousand homosexuals known
to the police; cf. Hirschfeld, *Die Homosexualität*, pp. 1000-1001 and

Homosexual Couple on the Battlefield

Rudolf Klare, *Homosexualität und Strafrecht* (Hamburg: Hanseatische Verlagsanstalt, 1937), p. 29. Hirschfeld was later sorely discredited within the homosexual community of Germany when it was revealed that he at least occasionally "leaked" information on homosexuals to the press; cf. *JfsZ* X (1909) 10.

7. A complete bibliography appears at the end of Hirschfeld's *Geschlechtskunde*, vol. 4 (Stuttgart: Julius Püttmann, 1930).

8. *JfsZ* I (1899) 139-165.

9. August Bebel's complete speech of January 13, 1898, appears in Germany, Reichstag, *Stenographische Berichte über die Verhandlungen*, 9th Legislative Session (1897-98), vol. 1, p. 410. An excerpt in English appears in John Lauritsen and David Thorstad, *The Early Homosexual Rights Movement (1864-1935)* (New York: Times Change Press, 1974), p. 13. As early as 1884, Bebel had written in his *Die Frau und der Sozialismus*:

> Yet another evil, frequently met, must also be shortly touched upon. Excessive sexual indulgence is infinitely more harmful than too little. . . . The number of young and old *roues* is enormous, and they require special irritants, excess having deadened and surfeited them. Many, accordingly, lapse into the unnatural practices of Greek days. The crime against nature is to-day much more general than most of us dream of; upon that subject the secret archives of many a Police Bureau could publish frightful information. But not among men only, among women also have the unnatural practices of old Greece come up again with force. . . . In Berlin, one-fourth of the prostitutes are said to practice "tribady;" but also in the circles of our leading dames there are not wanting disciples of Sappho. Still another unnatural gratification of the sexual instinct manifests itself in the violation of children. . . .

Quoted from August Bebel, *Woman Under Socialism*, transl. Daniel De Leon (New York: Labor News Press, 1904), pp. 164-165.

In his 1907 speech on the Eulenburg scandal, reprinted in *JfsZ* IX (1908) 634-637, Bebel still spoke in much the same terms as in 1884:

> The Chancellor said yesterday that these events were not a documentation of the decay of bourgeois society. That I will grant, *to a certain extent.* What we today are witnessing to an increased extent, and deplore, was once also widespread in Greece and elsewhere. One therefore speaks of Greek love, just as the similar love of the female sex is called Lesbian love. We now have Greek and Lesbian love in the German Reich, but ours is not a Periclean age.

Ibid., p. 636; emphasis added.

10. Hirschfeld, *Die Homosexualität*, p. 974.

11. The final list of names appeared in *JfsZ* XXIII (1923) 228-235. Among the first signers were Gerhart Hauptmann, Rainer Maria Rilke, and (the name that meant most to Hirschfeld) Richard von Krafft-Ebing. They were later joined by George Grosz, Martin Buber, Karl Jaspers, Hermann Hesse, Thomas and Heinrich Mann, Stefan Zweig, Arthur Schnitzler, Lou Andreas-Salomé, and Carl Maria Weber.

12. *Die Neue Zeit* XX/2 (1901-02) 89. The refusal of the Committee to challenge Christian morality is at least partly explained by Hirschfeld's own religion, monism. A peculiar metaphysical system elaborated by Hirschfeld's teacher, Ernst Haeckel (who was also the popularizer of Darwin's ideas in Germany), monism posited a grandly conceived evolution as the only force unfolding in history but explicitly retained the ethics of Christianity as the most advanced and appropriate for modern Europe. Hirschfeld explained in *JfsZ* VI (1904) 722: "We can say with a good conscience that we have to this day never given anyone occasion to feel injured in his religious or religio-ethical convictions by our activities. Nothing could be further from us than to violate the territory of the Church. . . ."

13. Hirschfeld, *Die Homosexualität*, p. 974.

14. *JfsZ* V/2 (1903) 1303   15. *Ibid.*, pp. 1308, 1309.

16. *Ibid.*, p. 1303.   17. *Ibid.*, p. 1320.

18. *JfsZ* VI (1904) 170.

19. Germany, Reichstag, *Protokolle*, vol. 204, p. 5829.

20. *Ibid.*, p. 5839. The entire debate is reprinted in the "Jahresbericht" of *JfsZ* VIII (1906) 1035 ff. Additional English excerpts appear in Lauritsen and Thorstad, *op. cit.*, p. 61. Cf. also Adolf Thiele, "Die Homosexualität in der Gesetzgebung," *Sozialistische Monatshefte* XIII (1909) 1486-1493 and "Kann Homosexualität strafbar sein?", *ibid.*, pp. 1560-1567.

21. Hirschfeld, *op. cit.*, p. 1003. Self-denunciation was viewed as one of the major "ethical tasks" of homosexuals by Kurt Hiller; cf. his "Ethische Aufgaben der Homosexuellen," *JfsZ* XIII (1912) 399-410, reprinted in his *Paragraph 175: Die Schmach des Jahrhunderts!* (Hanover: Paul Steegemann, 1922). Another advocate of mass denunciations was the anarchist Erich Mühsam, who is likely the bisexual "case study" presented on pp. 28-29 of his *Die Homosexualität: Ein Beitrag zur Sittengeschichte unserer Zeit*

(Berlin: M. Lilienthal, 1905); cf. Richard Linsert, *Kabale und Liebe: Über Politik und Geschlechtsleben* (Berlin: Man Verlag, 1931), p. 155.

22. Eulenburg had in 1884 published a homoerotic short story entitled "Aus der Art" in the literary journal *Nord und Süd* (vol. XXVIII) which turned on the notion of homosexuality as hereditary degeneracy; he was an advocate of Arthur Gobineau's social Darwinism and here applied it to homosexuality. The story remained undiscussed at the time of the scandals, when Eulenburg was mocked primarily because of his *Rosenlieder* and *Skaldengesänge*. This accounts for some of the details in the cartoon on page 36.

23. *JfsZ* X (1909) 7.   24. *JfsZ* XI (1910-11) 248.

25. Anna Rüling noted this in her speech, "Welches Interesse hat die Frauenbewegung an der Lösung des homosexuellen Problems?", *JfsZ* VII/1 (1905) 129-152. It was also discussed by Wilhelm Ham-hamer in *Die Tribadie Berlins* (Berlin: Hermann Seemann, 1906) and in "Ueber gleichgeschlechtliche Frauenliebe mit besonderer Berück-sichtigung der Frauenbewegung," *Monatsschrift für Harnkrankheiten und sexuelle Hygiene* IV (1907).

26. *JfsZ* VII/1 (1905) 147.

27. Hirschfeld reported that women played an active role in the Committee beginning in 1901: *JfsZ* IV (1902) 975. He also reported that police occasionally prevented women from attending the Committee's public forums, presumably because discussion of homosexuality was regarded as unsuitable for mixed company: *JfsZ* VIII (1906) 919.

28. *JfsZ* XI (1910-11) 256.   29. *Ibid.*, p. 257.

30. Quoted in *ibid.*, pp. 7-8.

31. Benedict Friedländer, *Renaissance des Eros Uranios* (Berlin-Schmargendorf: Verlag "Renaissance" Otto Lehmann, 1904), p. 258.

32. *Ibid.*, p. 259.   33. *JfsZ* XXIII (1923) 190.

34. Max Stirner's anarchism is criticized in Marx' and Engels' *The German Ideology* (1846); the views of Dühring are refuted in Engels' *Anti-Dühring* (1878). Friedländer's explicitly political works are *Der freiheitliche Sozialismus im Gegensatz zum Staats-knechtstum der Marxisten* (Berlin: Freie Verlagsanstalt, 1892) and *Die vier Hauptrichtungen der modernen sozialen Bewegung* (Berlin:

S. Calvary, 1901). He also comments on Marxism in his *Renais-sance*, p. 319. Contributors to *Der Eigene*, however, had diverse political views; one, Paul Harald Grävell, also wrote for *Ostara*, the Nordic and male supremacist journal which Hitler so admired.

35. Friedländer, *Renaissance*, p. 302. The Scientific-Human-itarian Committee was not untouched by the nudity movement. Hirsch-feld served as medical advisor to a nudist camp in Berlin-Grunewald beginning in 1906. Kurt Hiller describes his first experience in a nude athletics camp in rhapsodic terms in his *Leben gegen die Zeit,* vol. 2, *Eros* (Reinbek bei Hamburg: Rowohlt, 1973), pp. 40-45.

36. Friedländer, *op. cit.*, p. 300. Recent research has shown that an emphasis on naturalness frequently appears as a theme in the apologetics of contemporary German pedophiles. More-over, pedophiles tend to marry far more frequently than other homosexuals. The statistics and a Freudian interpretation appear in Martin Dannecker and Reimut Reiche, *Der gewöhnliche Homosexuelle* (Frankfurt am Main: Fischer, 1974), pp. 284-296.

37. See footnote 21.

38. I have been unable to consult the writings of "Sagitta" (Mackay), which are exceptionally rare. The reader should consult Thomas A. Riley, *Germany's Poet-Anarchist John Henry Mackay* (New York: Revisionist Press, 1972), pp. 104-114, for further informa-tion.

39. Friedländer, *op. cit.*, p. 66.

40. Quoted in Friedländer, *Denkschrift verfasst für die Freunde und Fondszeichner des Wissenschaftlich-Humanitären Komi-tees* (Berlin: By the author, 1907), p. 47. A playwright and poet, Kupffer documented his vehement anti-Marxism in *3000 Jahre Bol-schewismus* (Leipzig: Klaristischer Verlag Akropolis, 1920).

41. "Ein bisher ungedrucktes Kapitel aus der Entdeckung der Seele von Prof. Dr. Gustav Jaeger," *JfsZ* II (1900) 53-125.

42. Friedländer, *op. cit.*, p. 36.

43. *Ibid.*, p. 41.

44. *JfsZ* IX (1908) 629. Under attack from Friedländer and Freud, Hirschfeld quietly dropped the notion of a third sex in about 1910. Hirschfeld's scientific theories are far too complex to be dealt with here; the interested reader should consult Ralf Seidel, *Sexologie als positive Wissenschaft und sozialer Anspruch: Zur Sexualmorphologie Magnus Hirschfelds* (Munich: M.D. diss., 1969).

68

45. *Jahrbuch für die geistige Bewegung* III (1912) vi-vii.

46. Kurt Hildebrandt, *Norm Entartung Verfall* (Berlin: Verlag Die Runde, 1934), p. 207.

47. Friedländer's anti-clericalism is documented throughout his *Renaissance*. His anti-feminism is particularly pronounced in *Männliche und weibliche Kultur* (Berlin-Treptow: Bernhard Zack, 1908), a comparison of a supposedly effeminized America with a brutally masculine Japan. Shortly before his death in 1908, Friedländer penned "Seven Theses on Homosexuality." One thesis was:

> The erotic and social presumption of women is our enemy.
> Behind this presumption one often finds the wiles of
> priests or some other caste of cheats who make sly use
> of these gullible creatures with their small and simple
> brains. (*JfsZ* X (1909) 13.)

Friedländer's anti-feminism should be seen in the larger context of contemporary German society, whose middle class tended to view the concept of equality as a leftist political slogan, certainly not as a self-evident principle or a biological given. Friedländer was part of a much larger wave of reaction against the feminist movement.
    His anti-clericalism, on the other hand, was largely borrowed from the Young Hegelians (notably Stirner), who propounded the fallacious notion that the Christian religion was responsible for Germany's backwardness. The Young Hegelians concluded that a critique of Christianity was the primary (or at least a major) task in the effort for social change; they cherished the illusion that as the authors of this critique they were the vanguard of progressivism in Germany--a notion which was closely tied to contempt for the masses and a rejection of popular revolution. Friedländer adopted these ideas and applied them in a critique of the Christian taboo on homosexuality.

48. Cf. Brian Reade, *Sexual Heretics: Male Homosexuality in English Literature from 1850 to 1900* (New York: Coward-McCann, 1970), pp. 4-6.

49. Howard Becker, *German Youth: Bond or Free* (New York: Oxford University Press, 1946) and Walter Z. Laqueur, *Young Germany* (London: Routledge & Kegan Paul, 1962).

50. Quoted in Fritz Jungmann, "Autorität und Sexualmoral in der freien bürgerlichen Jugendbewegung," *Studien über Autorität und Familie,* ed. Max Horkheimer (Paris: Félix Alcan, 1936), p. 676.

51. *Ibid.*, p. 672.   52. *JfsZ* XXIII (1923) 189.

53. *JfsZ* XV (1915) 4. Prior to the outbreak of war, Germany was caught up in a militaristic mood which had a certain impact on the homosexual emancipation movement: at least two movement writers asked whether homosexuals made good soldiers; their answer was resoundingly in the affirmative. Cf. Friedländer, "Schadet die soziale Freigabe des homosexuellen Verkehrs der kriegerischen Tüchtigkeit einer Rasse?", *JfsZ* VII/1 (1905) 463-470, and Karl Franz von Leexow, *Armee und Homosexualität: Schadet Homosexualität die militärische Tüchtigkeit einer Rasse?* (Leipzig: Max Spohr, 1908).

54. Rudolf Klare, *Homosexualität und Strafrecht* (Hamburg: Hanseatische Verlagsanstalt, 1937), p. 30.

55. *JfsZ* XV (1915) 34.

CHAPTER III

THE STRUGGLE FOR A NATIONAL MOVEMENT

1919 - 1932

Over eight million soldiers lost their lives in World War I,
but Germany's capitulation on October 3, 1918, did not end the
bloodshed. Mutiny broke out in the German navy one month later,
and workers throughout the country went on strike in support of
the rebellion. On November 7, a council of workers, peasants,
and soldiers proclaimed the Republic of Bavaria. The revolutionary wave rapidly converged on Berlin, where a free (socialist)
republic was proclaimed on November 9. The Kaiser abdicated the
following day, and a rally in support of the Republic was held
in front of the Reichstag by the New Fatherland League (*Bund Neues
Vaterland*), an anti-monarchist peace organization which Hirschfeld
had joined in 1914. Hirschfeld spoke at the rally, which was interrupted at points by machine-gun fire from a nearby battle
between officers loyal to the Kaiser and the Red Guard. Hirschfeld concluded his speech with these words:

> There on the Reichstag stands the simple dedication: "For
> the German people." Up until three years ago that tablet
> was empty. The Kaiser had forbidden the inscription; it
> did not agree with his notions of divine right and sub-
> mission. In the future, the will of the king can never
> again be the supreme law. Instead, everything will be by
> the people and for the people! Together with a true

people's state with a genuinely democratic structure, we
want a social republic. Socialism means solidarity, community, reciprocity, the further development of society
into a unified body of people. . . . Before our mind's
eye pass the great pioneers of the Social Democracy who
could not witness this day: Ferdinand Lassalle, Karl Marx
and Friedrich Engels, August Bebel, Wilhelm Liebknecht,
and Paul Singer. . . . Citizens! Let us trust the new
Republican government; let each person help to maintain
calm and order. Then we will soon be able to lead again
lives of human dignity in peace. . . . Long live the
free German Republic! (1)

Hirschfeld had every reason to be hopeful at the prospect
of a socialist republic in Germany: just one year earlier, the
Czarist regime had been toppled in Russia, and within two months
of coming to power the Soviet Republic had done away with all
anti-homosexual legislation--an action which was to be reaffirmed
in the Soviet penal codes of 1922 and 1926.[2] But the interim
regime of the new German Republic, divided between Social Democrats and radical socialists, could not agree to follow the
Bolshevik model. Hirschfeld's own sympathies in fact lay firmly
with the right wing of the Social Democratic Party, with which
he was affiliated from 1898 until the time of his emigration.
A stalemate developed, and the radicals withdrew from the government; under the leadership of Karl Liebknecht and Rosa Luxemburg,
the Spartacus League (*Spartakus Bund*) moved to topple the regime,
but the attempt was bloodily crushed by the remnants of the German
military machine, now acting under the banner of the Republic.
The official who had commanded this measure, Friedrich Ebert,
received a letter of congratulations from the Scientific-Humanitarian Committee upon his election in 1919 to the chancellorship

of the Weimar Republic.[3] Later that year, a draft penal code
was brought before the Reichstag which discarded the penalization
of lesbian acts proposed in 1909 but set the maximum penalty for
male homosexual acts at five years. Germany was now a parliamentary democracy, but the revolution had been aborted. The homosexual emancipation movement was to spend another decade pressing
for penal reform.

The leading role in this legal struggle was filled by Kurt
Hiller (1885-1972), who joined the Scientific-Humanitarian Committee in 1908 and rose to become its co-chairperson in the late
twenties.[4] Hiller, who had a doctorate in law from the university of Heidelberg, was a vehement anti-Marxist throughout his
long career as a political essayist. His writings--he published
more than twenty books (including a volume of homoerotic verse)
and edited the political journal *Das Ziel* (The Goal) from 1916
to 1924--document his firm opposition to war, military conscription, and parliamentary democracy. Hiller coined the word activ-
ist, at least for the German language *(Aktivist)*, and he enjoyed
considerable respect in literary circles for his contributions
to the Expressionist movement.

A short time after joining the board of directors of the
Scientific-Humanitarian Committee in 1918, Hiller described the
political consciousness of contemporary homosexuals in these
terms:

A leader in the liberation struggle, an experienced man
who knows what he's talking about, recently assured me

that seventy-five percent of those interested in the
struggle in Germany favor the rightist parties, re-
storation of the monarchy, and revanchism. Only about
a quarter of those involved favor the Weimar Republic
or communism. (5)

Despite his own support for the Republic, Hiller advocated the

absolute neutrality of the emancipation movement:

The royalist must be just as welcome a helper as the
socialist republican, the strict Catholic as welcome as
the anarchistic freethinker, the communist as the bourgeois democrat. (6)

As a result, Hiller was quite willing to cooperate with repre-

sentatives of the Community of the Special and a new organization,

the German Friendship Association, in the formation of a national

Action Committee *(Aktionsausschuss)* in 1920.

The German Friendship Association *(Deutscher Freundschafts-*

Verband) was founded by Hans Kahnert and institutionalized the

dissatisfaction felt by many homosexuals about the academic orien-

tation of the Scientific-Humanitarian Committee and the elitism

of the Community of the Special. The Association attempted to

meet the needs of homosexuals who had neither scientific nor lit-

erary pretensions: it opened an activities center in Berlin, and

it held weekly meetings, sponsored dances, and published a weekly

newspaper entitled *Die Freundschaft* (Friendship). The Associa-

tion's approach to homosexual emancipation was an immediate and

lasting success: its second annual conference was attended by

forty-two delegates from chapters throughout Germany.[7] The

founding of the Association was initially welcomed by the Scien-

tific-Humanitarian Committee, which was able to use the pages

Kurt Hiller

of *Die Freundschaft* to publicize its own activities and expected

the Association to carry some of the burden of the legal struggle.

But concern increased that the resources of the movement were

being divided and that the Association was no more than a social

organization.

The Action Committee issued an appeal "to the homosexuals

of Germany" in January of 1921, urging them to become more involved

in the struggle for legal reform:

> Homosexuals, you know what the reasons and motives of your
> opponents amount to. You also know that your leaders and
> advocates have toiled untiringly for decades to banish
> prejudice, to disseminate truth, to win the rights due
> you--and these efforts have not been entirely unsuccess-
> ful. But in the final analysis, you yourselves must win
> your rights. Justice for you will finally be the fruit
> of your efforts alone. The liberation of homosexuals
> can only be the work of homosexuals themselves. (8)

This appeal was apparently ignored by both unmobilized homosexuals

and the steadily increasing number of local "friendship leagues"

(Freundschaftsbünde), whose relations with the Committee were

characterized by conflicting goals and--in the carefully selected

words of Kahnert--"a certain rivalry."[9]

The next national conference of the Friendship Association

was held on the Easter weekend of 1922, and it produced a flurry

of manifestos and leaflets, including one that was clearly inspired

by the Action Committee:

> Homosexuals of Hamburg!
>   Remember your duty and join us! On the 16th and 17th
> of April, the Second Congress of the Friendship Associa-
> tion will be meeting here: we must demonstrate that we
> have learned to win our human rights ourselves and have
> created an organization which demands respect. We no

longer want only a few scientists struggling for our
cause, we want to demonstrate our strength ourselves.
Here we stand, demanding that which is our right--and
who would dare to challenge us? For this reason, we
must work steadily and everyone must take part in our
work. No homosexual should be absent--rich or poor,
worker or scholar, diplomat or businessman. We cannot deprive ourselves of any support. Therefore join
us, swell our ranks before it is too late. At Easter
we must show whether we have developed into a fighting
organization or just a social club. He who does not
march with us marches against us. (10)

The conflict within the Association over social and political

ends was finally resolved in 1923, when the organization discon-

tinued its involvement in the legal reform struggle and, para-

doxically enough, also changed its name to the League for Human

Rights *(Bund für Menschenrecht)*.

If the Scientific-Humanitarian Committee was thus restored

to its position as the leading political organization within the

movement, the Community of the Special was increasingly challenged

in its publishing domain: *Die Freundschaft* changed from a weekly

to a monthly journal and increasingly focused upon literary and

cultural matters. A third journal entitled *Uranos*[11] also competed

with *Der Eigene*. The Scientific-Humanitarian Committee rejected

the "common opinion that the existence of such a large number of

relevant newspapers and magazines would mean a splintering of

our resources,"[12] but it was precisely the Committee's *Jahrbuch*

which was forced to discontinue publication by the notorious

hyperinflation which struck Germany in 1923. This is unfortunate

for a number of reasons, not the least of which is the *Jahrbuch*'s

value as the most accessible source of information on the movement as a whole. For the years 1924 to 1933, information about the movement is difficult to locate and sketchy at best.

There are tantalizingly few facts, and it is fortunate that Hirschfeld provided a brief overview of the situation in 1927:

> Since 1919, the so-called "homosexual press" has played a certain role. To be sure, there were some periodicals which appeared even earlier, such as Adolf Brand's *Der Eigene*--intellectually a top-flight production. But since the war, there has been an absolute tidal wave of homosexual journals, although in our opinion there is really no excuse for some of them. One of the culturally significant journals which unfortunately no longer appears was *Uranos,* which was particularly notable for its high literary quality. Another is *Die Freundschaft,* which took an activist stance in the years 1921-23 and succeeded for a time in mobilizing the homosexual masses. The extent to which its current, purely literary orientation has been determined by its readership is beyond our knowledge. But *Die Freundschaft* does deserve credit for scrupulously avoiding the in-fighting and backbiting between individual groups and goals that has become typical of the movement as a whole. (13)

Hirschfeld named only three of the thirty periodicals for homosexuals which appeared during the Weimar Republic.[14] Although a few editors had occasional difficulties with the law (as had Adolf Brand during the Wilhelmine era), the elimination of prepublication censorship and the greater freedom of the press brought a "tidal wave" of commercial speculation in publishing.

The wide distribution of homophile literature, including works of fiction, was accompanied by a decrease in the number of non-fiction books on the subject. In some respects, it appears that the almost legendary flowering of the homosexual subculture during the heyday of the "Golden Twenties" worked to the detriment of the emancipation movement: a contradiction between

HOMOSEXUAL PERIODICALS OF THE 1920s

Among these periodicals is the only known picture of *Friendship and Freedom,* published by the Chicago Society for Human Rights (1924-25). Inspired by the German movement and founded by Henry Gerber, this was the earliest documented homosexual emancipation organization in the United States. Two issues of *Friendship and Freedom* are said to have been printed; no copies are now known to exist.

Lesbian Bar of the "Golden Twenties"

personal and collective liberation emerged, for it was far
easier to luxuriate in the concrete utopia of the urban sub-
culture than to struggle for an emancipation which was apparently
only formal and legalistic.[15] Official tolerance was manifested,
for example, in the unhindered consumption of narcotics in some
homosexual bars,[16] and transvestites were issued police certifi-
cates permitting them to crossdress in public.[17] The great
debate over cultural and political lines which had occurred
during the Wilhelmine era gave way to "infighting and backbiting"
(*innerer Zwist und Hader*) and countless manifestations of spe-
cialized interests. To name only two: the first homosexual theater group, *Theater des Eros*, was founded in Berlin-Steglitz on
July 6, 1921, by Bruno Mattusek[18]; in 1928, a physician named
Karl-Günter Heimsoth, later a Nazi sympathizer, published an
elaborate tome on homosexuality and astrology.[19]

The twenties also brought discussion of the feasibility of
forming a national homosexual political party,[20] for the terms
of Article 17 of the constitution of the Weimar Republic permit-
ted any minority which could muster 60,000 votes to constitute
a national party and to seat a representative in the Reichstag.
But Hirschfeld noted in 1927:

> The events of the year 1918 have doubtless had a certain
> effect on the liberation struggle of homosexuals, even
> though the goal of the ongoing penal reform efforts has
> not been reached. For beyond the groups of humane and
> just scientists, homosexual organizations have arisen
> along the lines of special-interest groups or unions and
> have taken up the struggle for their fellows. Without

wishing to question the justification of these attempts
or the desirability of their ultimate success, it should
be stated that all the efforts aimed at creating a "mass
organization" of homosexuals have, in the end, failed.
It is untrue that homosexuals form a sort of "secret
society" among themselves with all sorts of code sig-
nals and mutual defense arrangements. Aside from a few
minor cliques, homosexuals are in reality almost totally
lacking in feelings of solidarity; in fact, it would be
difficult to find another class of mankind which has
proved so incapable of organizing to secure its basic
legal and human rights. (21)

The note of disappointment in this commentary stems from the fact

that most organizations of the twenties avoided political issues

and focused instead on arranging social events.

One can only speculate as to the number of homosexual groups

in existence when Hirschfeld wrote his commentary. It is likely

that the number of organizations increased rapidly in the early

years of the Weimar Republic and then reached a plateau or con-

tinued to increase at a slower rate. As early as 1923, there

were at least twenty-five organizations, but information on them

is quite sketchy. For example: in Berlin, the *Bund der Freunde

und Freundinnen* (League of Friends) held conferences on scientific,

literary, and artistic subjects and also organized social events;

the Munich chapter of the German Friendship Association was forced

to disband by constant Nazi harassment; the Hamburg Society for

Scientific Research was divided into two sections, one for men

and one for lesbians. Other organizations were located in Braun-

schweig, Breslau, Kassel, Krefeld, Düsseldorf, Eisenach, Weimar,

Frankfurt am Main, Karlsruhe, Leipzig, Saarbrücken, Dortmund, Dres-

den, Oberhausen, Lübeck, and other cities.[22]

Despite the failure of the national Action Committee, Kurt
Hiller remained more or less closely involved with the "ongoing
penal code reform efforts" mentioned by Hirschfeld. In 1922,
a highly progressive code was drafted by the Minister of Justice,
Gustav Radbruch, a Social Democrat who had been Hiller's law
teacher at the university of Heidelberg and had signed the Scientific-Humanitarian Committee's petition; but Radbruch did not
succeed in bringing this draft before the Reichstag. In 1925,
the Reichstag was presented with a second, unsigned draft which
Hiller described in his customary acidulous style as "the super-
idioitic high (or, if you will, low) point of bigotry."[23] The
response was the formation of a Coalition for Reform of the Sexual
Crimes Code (*Kartell für Reform des Sexualstrafrechts*), which
set about drafting a comprehensive alternative under Hiller's
direction. One of Hiller's co-workers in the Coalition was the
communist lawyer Felix Halle, who elsewhere provided a clear for-
mulation of the German Communist Party's approach to homosexuality:

> The class-conscious proletariat, uninfluenced by the ideo-
> logy of property and freed from the ideology of the churches,
> approaches the question of sex life and also the problem of
> homosexuality with a lack of prejudice afforded by an under-
> standing of the overall social structure. . . . In accord-
> ance with the scientific insights of modern times, the pro-
> letariat regards these relations as a special form of sexual
> gratification and demands the same freedom and restrictions
> for these forms of sex life as for intercourse between the
> sexes, i.e. protection of the sexually immature from attacks,
> . . . control over one's own body, and finally respect for
> the rights of non-involved parties. (24)

The Coalition consisted of seven organizations, but only one--
the Scientific-Humanitarian Committee--was a homosexual group.[25]

Discouraged by the non-political stance of nearly all homosexual organizations, Hiller had come to realize that "no matter how critical, no matter how constructive, a self-imposed limitation to Paragraph 175 would be ineffective."[26] Hiller credited the Coalition's draft, which was published as a small book in 1927, with a degree of influence on the Reichstag deliberations in 1928 and 1929.

In 1928, all German political parties were canvassed by Adolf Brand as to their views on penal reform and reform of Paragraph 175 in particular. The views of the Nazi Party were expressed in no uncertain terms:

Suprema lex salus populi!
Community before individual!   Munich, 14 May 1928
    It is not necessary that you and I live, but it is necessary that the German people live. And it can only live if it can fight, for life means fighting. And it can only fight if it maintains its masculinity. It can only maintain its masculinity if it exercises discipline, especially in matters of love. Free love and deviance are undisciplined. Therefore we reject you, as we reject anything which hurts our people.
    Anyone who even thinks of homosexual love is our enemy. We reject anything which emasculates our people and makes it a plaything for our enemies, for we know that life is a fight and it's madness to think that men will ever embrace fraternally. Natural history teaches us the opposite. Might makes right. And the stronger will always win over the weak. Let's see to it that we once again become the strong! But this we can only do in one way--the German people must once again learn how to exercise discipline. We therefore reject any form form of lewdness, especially homosexuality, because it robs us of our last chance to free our people from the bondage which now enslaves it. (27)

The German Communist Party answered the same question:

                                        Berlin, 7 May 1928
    In response to your letter of May 5, let us simply
    state that the CP has always carried on the most resolute

struggle for the repeal of Paragraph 218 (the law pro-
hibiting abortion). . . .
      The CP has also taken a stand for the repeal of Para-
graph 175 at every available opportunity. We need
simply remind you of the recent [Reichstag] debate on
the law for fighting venereal disease as well as the
debate of the [Reichstag] Committee for Penal Code
Reform. There is no need to emphasize that we will
continue to wage the most resolute struggle for the
repeal of these laws in the future. (28)

In 1929, the Communist Party was represented on the Reichstag

Committee for Penal Code Reform by the delegate Maslowski.

Following the example set by the Soviet Union, Maslowski joined

with the delegates of the Social Democratic and German Democratic

Parties in voting to strike Paragraph 175 from the German penal

code.

      The legalization of homosexual acts between consenting adults

in private was approved by a committee vote of fifteen to thirteen

on October 16, 1929. The event was celebrated by both the homo-

sexual emancipation movement and unmobilized homosexuals through-

out the country. Formal adoption of the Penal Code Reform Bill

by the full Reichstag--the goal toward which the movement had been

working for thirty-two years--seemed within grasp when the American

stock market crash intervened. The ensuing crisis strained the

Reichstag to the limit, and the bill was tabled, never to be taken

up again: 1929 marked the turning point in the Nazi rise to power.

      The Nazis were later to develop their own variety of sexual

reform on the basis of eugenics: the extermination of homosexuals,

Jews, the retarded, and the deformed as well as various other

measures were a totally serious effort to improve the Aryan race.

Prior to its fascist perversion, however, eugenics was one of
three movements within the overall sexual reform effort, the
other two being the birth control movement and the sexual emancipation movement. (The homosexual emancipation movement was
only one wing within the latter.) Although these three movements began with a unified ideology, they clearly split during
the years of the Weimar Republic, the eugenics movement going
to the right, the sexual emancipation movement to the left, and
the birth control movement to the center. As these internal
divisions widened, the non-partisan stance of the broader sexual
reform effort became ever more precarious, and it was finally
sundered in 1935. The relevant developments within the homosexual
emancipation movement have been traced above, and the following
chapter will treat Nazi eugenics as applied to homosexuality.
Finally, the career of Magnus Hirschfeld exemplified the perilous
futility of clinging to detached, scientific neutrality in an
increasingly polarized political climate.

In 1918, Hirschfeld's birthday was marked by the appearance
of a festschrift edited by Georg Plock, the secretary of the Scientific-Humanitarian Committee.[29] At fifty, Hirschfeld could look
back on twenty-five years as a medical practitioner and twenty-one
years as the sole nationally recognized figure of the homosexual
movement. He was fond of quoting the constant admonition of one
of his science teachers, "Observe, gentlemen, observe," and the
thousands of case histories he had accumulated as a clinician

and as a homosexual leader had gone into the preparation of two major works, *Die Homosexualität des Mannes und des Weibes* (Male and Female Homosexuality, 1914) and *Die Transvestiten: Eine Untersuchung über den erotischen Verkleidungstrieb* (Transvestites: A Study of Erotic Disguise, 1910). Hirschfeld himself was both a homosexual and a transvestite (a word he coined), and these works were in some sense apologetics; but they were also monumentally comprehensive collections of (still useful) data on their subjects.

The publication of these volumes helped to salvage Hirschfeld's reputation, which had been nearly destroyed by his appearance in the Moltke *vs.* Harden trial. Anti-Semites proved particularly unforgiving about this incident: part of the *Dolchstosslegende* (which attributed German defeat in World War I to a "stab in the back" by Jewish interests on the homefront) maintained that morale had been weakened by the knowledge that the enemy regarded "the entire German army as inverted."[30] Hirschfeld never concerned himself with the Jewish question, except to rebut in passing the notion that the percentage of homosexuals was lower among Jews than among other groups.[31] In 1914, Hirschfeld gave one of a series of lectures on the war with the title, "Why Do the Peoples Hate Us?" "Us" referred neither to Jews nor to homosexuals, but to Germans-- perhaps the least interesting question of all.

As soon as the Weimar Republic was established, Hirschfeld once again placed himself firmly in the public eye by appearing in a film--the first homosexual emancipation film. Entitled

Anders als die Andern (Different from the Others), this "six-act,"
feature-length, silent film was produced and directed by Richard
Oswald and starred Conrad Veidt (of *Caligari* fame), Fritz Schultz,
and Reinhold Schünzel.[33]   It told the story of a homosexual blackmail victim who eventually turned to Hirschfeld for aid.   The
film received restrained reviews, and one commentator noted:

> . . .the leading role was played by Conrad Veidt, who made
> a somewhat unhappy impression at the start as an adolescent
> in the then popular sailor suit. He fell into the clutches
> of a blackmailer who was so physically unappealing that the
> film by now was becoming rather unpersuasive to the detached
> observer. The highpoint was the appearance of the philan-
> thropic doctor, and this role was filled by Dr. Hirschfeld
> himself! It was all too understandable that this film left
> an unfavorable impression. . .and Dr. Hirschfeld's influence
> continued to wane. (34)

The film was first shown to the press on May 24, 1919, and it was
quickly banned in Munich, Stuttgart, and Vienna due to anti-Semitic
outbursts.   In Munich, Thomas Mann now referred to "Hirschfeld and
his ghastly Committee"[35]--although he had willingly signed the Committee's petition some years earlier.

Hirschfeld was assaulted by anti-Semites for the first time on
October 4, 1920, in Munich.   A Nazi commentator gleefully noted: "It
is not without charm to know that. . .Hirschfeld was so beaten that
his eloquent mouth could never again be kissed by one of his 'disci-
ples'."[36]   In 1921, he was again attacked in Munich and left for
dead with a fractured skull--his obituary even appeared prematurely
in some papers.   In 1923, a youth at a lecture in Vienna opened
fire on Hirschfeld, wounding several people in the audience.[37]
For the younger generation, the film was a first exposure to Hirsch-

Blackmail Scene from *Anders als die Andern*

feld altogether; a Nazi historian incorrectly noted:

> A certain decadence had already begun to infect German
> theatrical and artistic life prior to the war, primarily
> due to Jewish influence. But Jewish libertinism was kept
> within certain bounds by public order and police super-
> vision. . . . The chief domain of these money-grubbers
> was the film. In this area, Jewish commercial speculation
> celebrated absolute orgies with the commodity of indecency.
> . . . In the spring of 1919, two films stood out from
> the usual garbage and caused a special stir. With a mix-
> ture of shame and cunning, these were called "educational"
> films: we are referring to the films *Prostitution* and
> *Anders als die Andern*. . . . This was the first appear-
> ance of that man, Hirschfeld, who. . .has upon his con-
> science a good deal of the outrage at Jewish frivolity
> which was building up in the German people and which
> finally exploded in 1933. (38)

Hirschfeld was becoming the object of such animosity that when

the Coalition for Reform of the Sexual Crimes Code was constituted

in 1925, Hirschfeld was kept in the background by Kurt Hiller.

The Committee's work was increasingly taken over by Hiller and

his protégé Richard Linsert (1899-1933), a Trotskyist who had

joined the Committee as secretary in 1923. When the film *Anders*

als die Andern was remade as *Gesetze der Liebe* (Laws of Love) in

1927, the story and actors were virtually the same except that

Hirschfeld's role was eliminated and, in the absence of a *deus*

ex machina, the story ended with Veidt's suicide.

Despite the increasing politicization of the issue of homo-

sexual rights, Hirschfeld's Committee maintained the neutral stance

it had held from the outset. In its monthly newsletter (issued

after the demise of the *Jahrbuch*), this point was emphasized:

> The Scientific-Humanitarian Committee. . .well realizes that
> *it must be committed to the strictest non-partisan neutrality*
> *in its struggle,* proceeding from the consideration that ad-
> herents of all political views are included among its members. (39)

In July of 1927, after a Nazi Reichstag delegate made a speech attacking homosexuality and Hirschfeld, the newsletter made this appeal:

> We further feel obliged to urgently request of our numerous members in the National Socialist German Workers Party. . . that they vigorously call their delegates to order. (40)

It is difficult to understand why homosexuals were tolerated in the Nazi Party, which had openly anti-homosexual policies; but it is also difficult to grasp why members of the Nazi Party were tolerated in the homosexual emancipation movement.

In view of the "infighting and backbiting" within the homosexual movement and the mounting threats from without, it is not surprising that Hirschfeld gradually withdrew and devoted more of his time to the broader sexual reform movement, in which he was highly respected and far less controversial. On July 1, 1919, he realized one of his fondest dreams by opening the Institute of Sexual Science *(Institut für Sexualwissenschaft)* in Berlin. The building was purchased by Hirschfeld with his own funds, and he made a gift of it to the Prussian government in 1924. Staffed by four physicians and their assistants, the Institute housed both clinical and research facilities which were open to the public and visited by scientists from around the world.[42] In addition to offering marriage and career counseling, venereal disease testing and treatment, family planning and sex education programs, and psychiatric and physical therapy, the Institute had a library and museum that amassed unparalleled collections of biological, sociological, and ethnological materials. While they maintained autonomy,

the Scientific-Humanitarian Committee and World League for Sexual
Reform also had offices in the Institute. Based on the thousands
of consultations he gave at the Institute, Hirschfeld prepared his
magnum opus, *Sexualkunde* (Sexual Knowledge), which was published
in five volumes from 1926 to 1930.

The Berlin Institute became a center of the international
sexual reform movement when Hirschfeld convened the First Congress
for Sexual Reform. Held from September 15 to 20, 1921, the Congress was attended by leading world figures in such fields as law,
endocrinology, contraception, sex education, eugenics, and general
sexology. From this meeting emerged the World League for Sexual
Reform, of which Hirschfeld was a co-president; at its peak, the
organizations affiliated with the League had a combined membership
of 130,000. The succeeding conferences were held in Copenhagen
(1928), London (1929), and Vienna (1930).

The work of the League was just as threatened by the depression
and the rise of fascism as was the homosexual emancipation movement.
In a speech he delivered at the 1930 Congress, Wilhelm Reich criticized the League for avoiding these issues:

> The committee preparing the Fourth Congress of the World
> League for Sexual Reform has emphasized a concern for
> "sexual reform on a scientific basis" in its announcement.
> Since serious sexual reform cannot dispense with scienti-
> fically based conclusions, this emphasis would be purely
> superfluous were it not meant to imply a contrast to another
> standpoint—namely, a political one. Furthermore, this
> emphasis can only mean that political discussion is to be
> excluded from the conference. Although it is obvious that
> the fundamentals of sexual reform must be based upon
> science, I maintain that the primary issue to be clarified
> is the question as to whether the political relations of

Institute of Sexual Science, Berlin

FIRST CONGRESS FOR SEXUAL REFORM

(Berlin, 1921)

a given state or social system permit the practical implementation of scientific knowledge—in other words, whether or not sexual reform is actually possible under existing circumstances. (43)

Reich himself drew the consequences and organized the German Association for Proletarian Sexual Politics (*Deutscher Reichsverband für Proletarische Sexualpolitik*), known as Sexpol, the following year. The World League was disbanded in 1935 by its presidents, J. H. Leunbach of Denmark and Norman Haire of England, who were irreconcilably divided over the question raised by Reich in 1930.

After the Vienna Conference, Hirschfeld went abroad on a worldwide speaking tour which was to take him to the United States,[44] Japan, China, Indonesia, India, and Palestine; his experiences formed the basis for a book, *Die Weltreise eines Sexualforschers* (The World Journey of a Sexologist, 1933). But by the time he returned to Europe, the Nazi Party had made such gains that Hirschfeld found it advisable not to enter Germany, and he remained in Paris. The last book Hirschfeld was able to have published in Germany, *Sittengeschichte der Nachkriegszeit* (Manners and Morals of the Post—War Era, 1932), closed with a hastily written and moving postscript which is worth quoting *in extenso*:

The times in which the appearance of our second volume falls prompt us to an aside, a closing note which will also serve to explain why it is that we consider the history of of the post—war period at an end, not only on these pages but also in reality. The depression now afflicting the entire world, probably the most terrible crisis since a world economy has come into being, suggests to us this thought: if the post—war period (of and by itself a significant term) is the designation for a specific historical epoch and not merely a name for all the years which have followed and will follow the World War, then this post—war period *already*

Magnus Hirschfeld

belongs to past history. It lasted as long as the primary economic development—and correspondingly the political and ideological development as well—took place under the impact of that great struggle of nations. But this was the case as long as economics and ideology had to eliminate the accursed legacy of the war, as long as it was necessary to bury the dead, clear away the rubble, and recreate the productive forces of society which had been deranged, and in large measure destroyed, by the war. The years of need and underproduction (inflation) and the ensuing over-production (rationalization) can be clearly recognized in the post-war period, along with the new forms of human relations, including those between the sexes, which were possible only on that basis. The conditions which led to the present crisis certainly arose in those years, too, but the depression is not itself a legacy of the war; it is not another phase of the post-war period but its very conclusion and end. Simultaneously it is the beginning of a new period, which has received from its predecessor the economic crisis conjured up by post-war capitalism as an historic task—one which perhaps can no longer be solved by capitalism at all.

What is true for economic development is also true for the history of morals. This, too, is moving toward a new period, and we do not believe that this will properly be termed the post-war era. Presumably, and even probably, it will bring new forms of relations between the sexes of which we, the witnesses and modest chroniclers of the morals of the now historical post-war period, cannot even dream. (45)

NOTES

1. *Jahrbuch für sexuelle Zwischenstufen* XVIII (1918) 165-166; the *Jahrbuch* will hereafter be cited as *JfsZ*.

2. Dr. Grigorii Batkis, professor at the department of social hygiene of Moscow University, explained the basic principle of Soviet legislation in these terms: "It declares the absolute non-involvement of state and society in sexual relations provided they harm no one and infringe upon no one's interests. . . . Homosexuality, sodomy, and various other forms of sexual gratification set forth in European legislation as offenses against public morality are treated by Soviet legislation exactly as is so-called 'natural' intercourse. All forms of intercourse are private matters." *Die Sexualrevolution in Russland* (Berlin: Verlag Der Syndikalist Fritz Kater, 1925), pp. 6, 22.

3. *JfsZ* XVIII (1918) 173-175.

4. Kurt Hiller, *Leben gegen die Zeit,* vol. 1, *Logos* (Reinbek bei Hamburg: Rowohlt, 1969), pp. 73–74, and vol. 2, *Eros* (Reinbek bei Hamburg: Rowohlt, 1972), p. 90.

5. Hiller, *Paragraph 175: Die Schmach des Jahrhunderts!* (Hanover: Paul Steegemann, 1922), p. 78.

6. *Ibid.,* p. 79.   7. *JfsZ* XXIII (1923) 188.

8. *JfsZ* XXI (1921) 55. The final sentence of this excerpt clearly echoes the then standard slogan, "The liberation of the working class can only be the work of the working class itself."

9. *JfsZ* XXIII (1923) 187.

10. Quoted in Ambroise Got, "Le Vice organisé en Allemagne," *Mercure de France* CLXI (1923) 677. Got observed the German homosexual movement from his vantage point as military attaché at the French embassy in Berlin. See also his *L'Allemagne après le débâcle* (Strasbourg: Imprimerie Strasbourgeoise, 1919), pp. 220–227.

11. Karl Heinrich Ulrichs announced the plan to issue a journal entitled *Uranos* as early as 1869; cf. Magnus Hirschfeld, *Die Homosexualität des Mannes und des Weibes* (Berlin: Louis Marcus, 1914), p. 960.

12. *JfsZ* XXIII (1923) 242.

13. Hirschfeld, "Die Homosexualität," *Sittengeschichte des Lasters,* ed. Leo Schidrowitz (Vienna: Verlag für Kulturforschung, 1927), p. 310.

14. The following is a list of all German-language periodicals which appeared prior to the Third Reich; with the exception of the Committee's *JfsZ* and a few scattered volumes of Brand's *Der Eigene,* none are represented in the holdings of North American libraries:

Agathon (1917-18)
Die BiF: Blätter für ideale Frauenfreundschaften
Blätter für Menschenrecht (1919-21?)
Das dritte Geschlecht
Die Ehelosen
Der Eigene (1896-1929)
Extrapost
Eros (1927-30?)
Die Fanfare
Frauenliebe
Die freie Presse (1922?)
Der Freund
Die Freundin (1924-29)

Die Freundschaft (1919-23, 1929?)
Freundschaft und Freiheit (1921-?)
Das Freundschaftsblatt (1922-?)
Der Führer
Garconne (1925-30?)
Geissel und Rute (?)
Der Hellas-Bote
Die Insel (1925-30?)
Jahrbuch für sexuelle Zwischenstufen (1899-1923)
Der Kreis
Ledige Frauen
Der Merkur (1922)
Mitteilungen des Wissenschaftlich-humanitären Komitees
Monatsberichte des Wissenschaftlich-humanitären Komitees
Rundbrief (1925-?)
Die Sonne
Der Strom
Die Tante (1926?)
Uranos (1922-27)

15. Cf. David Fernbach, *The Rise and Fall of the Gay Liberation Front* (London: London School of Economics Gay Culture Society, 1973), for a similar analysis.

16. Got, *Mercure de France* CLXI (1923) 674-675.

17. Rudolf Klare, *Homosexualität und Strafrecht* (Hamburg: Hanseatische Verlagsanstalt, 1937), p. 33.

18. At least four playwrights wrote for the theater: Reinhold Kluge (*Wer ist schuld?*), Fredy Konradt (*Andere Liebe*), Élisàr von Kupffer (*Satire und Tragödie*), and Hans Wedell.

19. Heimsoth, *Charakterkonstellation mit besonderer Berücksichtigung der Gleichgeschlechtlichkeit* (Munich: Barth, 1928).

20. Cf. Kurt Hiller's essay, "Homosexualität und Proporz," in his *Paragraph 175* and the lead article of the January 14, 1927 issue of *Das Freundschaftsblatt*, "Homoerotische Freiheitspartei!" (reprinted in Klare, *op. cit.*, p. 147).

21. Hirschfeld, *op. cit.*, p. 309.

22. Got, *op. cit.*, pp. 655-678.

23. Hiller, *Logos*, p. 208.

24. Felix Halle, *Geschlechtsleben und Strafrecht* (Berlin: Mopr Verlag, 1931), pp. 72-73.

25. The other organizations were the *Abteilung für Sexual-reform am Institut für Sexualwissenschaft, Bund für Mutterschutz und Sexualreform, Deutsche Liga für Menschenrecht, Gesellschaft für Geschlechtskunde, Gesellschaft für Sexualreform*, and *Verband für Eherechtsreform*. Cf. Hiller, *Eros*, pp. 96-99.

26. Hiller, *Eros*, p. 97.

27. Klare, *op. cit.*, p. 114.

28. On the drastic change in communist policy beginning around 1932, see John Lauritsen and David Thorstad, *The Early Homosexual Rights Movement (1864-1935)* (New York: Times Change Press, 1974), pp. 68-70; Guy Hocquenghem, *Le Désir homosexuel* (Paris: Editions Universitaires, 1972), *passim*; and Thorsten Graf and Mimi Steglitz (pseuds.), "Homosexuellenunterdrückung in der bürgerlichen Gesellschaft," *Probleme des Klassenkampfs* IV (1974) 17-50.

29. The festschrift was issued as a double fascicle (April-July, 1918) of the *Vierteljahresberichte des Wissenschaftlich-Humanitären Komitees* (= *JfsZ* XVIII).

30. Klare, *op. cit.*, p. 30.

31. Hirschfeld, *Die Homosexualität*, p. 524.

32. The lecture appeared as a book: *Warum hassen uns die Völker?* (Bonn: Marcus & Weber, 1915); cf. Linsert, *Kabale und Liebe: Über Politik und Geschlechtsleben* (Berlin: Man Verlag, 1931), p. 157.

33. The only copy of this film known to have survived the Third Reich is now in East Berlin--with Russian subtitles.

34. Albrecht Dietrich Freiherr von Dieckhoff, *Zur Rechts-lage im derzeitigen Sittenstrafrecht* (Hamburg: Verlag für kriminalistische Fachliteratur, 1958), p. 93.

35. In a letter dated July 4, 1920, to Carl Maria Weber, another petition signer. It appears in his *Briefe*, vol. 1, *1899-1936*, ed. Erika Mann (Frankfurt am Main: S. Fischer, 1961), p. 180. In the same letter, a defense of *Der Tod in Venedig* against charges that it was anti-homosexual, Mann said he was pleased that Hiller liked the story while Hirschfeld did not. This may be a sign of his animus, for their views were exactly the opposite: cf. *JfsZ* XIV (1914) 338-341 for Hiller's opinion and *Die Homosexualität*, p. 1020 for Hirschfeld's. For other opinions of Mann on homosexuality, see the essay "Von deutscher Republik" (1922) in his *Gesammelte Werke* (Frankfurt am Main: S. Fischer,

1960), vol. 11, especially p. 847 and the essay "Über die Ehe" (1925), *ibid.*, vol. 10, especially pp. 196-199. Perhaps as a result of conflict with his children, Klaus and Erika, who were homosexual, Mann's views became increasingly negative.

36. Klare, *op. cit.*, p. 30.

37. This and other information on Hirschfeld appears in Max Hodann, *History of Modern Morals* (London: W. Heinemann, 1937), which gives a useful overview of the sexual reform movement.

38. Institut zum Studium der Judenfrage, *Die Juden in Deutschland* (Munich: n.p., 1939), pp. 371-372.

39. Quoted in Linsert, *op. cit.*, p. 156.

40. *Ibid.*

41. See, e.g., Stefan Waldecke (i.e., Ewald Tscheck), *Das Wissenschaftlich-Humanitäre Komitee: Warum ist es zu bekämpfen und sein Wirken schädlich für das deutsche Volk?* (Berlin: Adolf Brand, 1925).

42. William J. Robinson, "The Institute for Sexual Science --The Only Institution of Its Kind in the World," *Medical Critic and Guide* XXV (1925) 391-396. Impressed by his visit, Robinson remarked, "When I get back to New York, I may try to establish the first Institute of this kind in the U.S. . . ." (p. 396).

43. Wilhelm Reich, "Sexualnot der Werktätigen und die Schwierigkeit sexueller Beratung," *Sexualnot und Sexualreform: Verhandlungen der Weltliga für Sexualreform. . . .*, ed. Josef K. Friedjung et al. (Vienna: Elbemühl, 1931), p. 397. Cf. Anson Rabinbach, "The Politicization of Wilhelm Reich," *New German Critique* I (1974-75) 90-97 for the background of Reich's speech and a translation.

44. For the speech welcoming Hirschfeld to the American Society for Medical History, see Victor Robinson, "In Honor of Magnus Hirschfeld," *Anthropos* I/1 (1934) 49-51 (= *Medical Review of Reviews* #458). Robinson's *Encyclopedia Sexualis* (New York: Dingwall-Rock, 1936), pp. 317-321, contains a biography of Hirschfeld.

45. Hirschfeld, ed., *Sittengeschichte der Nachkriegszeit*, vol. 2 (Leipzig and Vienna: Verlag für Sexualwissenschaft, 1932), p. 397.

CHAPTER IV

THE FINAL SOLUTION

1933 - 1945

On January 30, 1933, Adolf Hitler was named chancellor of
Germany, an event celebrated by a massive torchlight parade of
SA troops through the center of Berlin. Hitler's coalition government, however, lacked a parliamentary majority, and new elections were therefore scheduled for March 5. The elections were
preceded, accompanied, and followed by outbursts of violence,
including the Reichstag fire of February 27, which was falla-
ciously attributed to the communists. The electorate's longing
for law and order resulted in a hairbreadth victory for the Nazi
Party, and the Thousand Year Reich had begun. Kurt Hiller's
apartment was invaded and searched by the SS on March 7, and he
was arrested on March 23; he was eventually sent to the concentration camp at Oranienburg. Through a fluke that Hiller himself
never understood, he was released after nine months and, on the
verge of death from brutal mistreatment, escaped to Prague and
later to London.[1]

On May 6, a Berlin newspaper announced that the city was to
be purged of un-German spirit by destroying objectionable books.
The first target of this campaign was Hirschfeld's Institute of

Sexual Science, described by the Nazis as "the international center of the white-slave trade"[2] and "an unparalleled breeding ground
of dirt and filth."[3] The staff at the Institute acted quickly, but
it was too late:

> An attempt was made to remove for safe-keeping some of the
> most valuable private books and manuscripts; but this proved
> impossible, as the person removing the books was arrested
> by a guard which had evidently been placed round the Insti-
> tute during the night. At 9:30 a.m. some lorries drew up
> in front of the Institute with about one hundred students
> and a brass band. They drew up in military formation in
> front of the Institute, and then marched into the building
> with their band playing. As the office was not yet open,
> there was no responsible person there; there were only a
> few women and one man. The students demanded entrance to
> every room, and broke in the doors of those which were closed,
> including the office of the World League for Sexual Reform.
> When they found that there was not much to be had in the
> lower rooms, they made their way up to the first floor,
> where they emptied the ink bottles over manuscripts and
> carpets and then made for the book-cases. They took away
> whatever they thought not completely unobjectionable, working
> for the most part on the basis of the so-called "black list."
> . . . .
> The staff was kept under observation during the whole of
> the proceedings, and the band played throughout, so that a
> large crowd of inquisitive people gathered outside. At 12
> o'clock the leader made a long speech, singing a particu-
> larly vulgar song and also the Horst-Wessel song.
> At three o'clock a number of truckloads of storm troop-
> ers showed up and announced that they were going to con-
> tinue the work begun that morning. The second troop then
> proceeded to make a careful search through every room,
> taking down to the lorries basket after basket of valua-
> ble books and manuscripts--two lorry-loads in all. . . .
> Many bound volumes of periodicals were also taken. They also
> wanted to take away several thousand questionnaires which
> were among the records, but desisted when they were assured
> that these were simply medical histories. On the other
> hand, it did not prove possible to dissuade them from
> removing the material belonging to the World League for
> Sexual Reform, the whole edition of the journal *Sexus*,
> and the card index. In addition, a great many manu-
> scripts, including many unpublished ones, fell into their
> hands. . . . (4)

More than 12,000 books were removed from the Institute's
library of 20,000 volumes, together with a large part of its
unique collection of 35,000 pictures. On May 10, these materials
were burned in a public ceremony, and a bust of Hirschfeld taken
from the Institute was held aloft and thrown into the fire. One
week later, Hirschfeld had the unusual sensation of seeing all this
in a newsreel shown in a Paris cinema; he wrote that it was like
watching his own funeral.[5] The Institute, which had been visited
by a quarter of a million people, was handed over to the use of
the Nazi Association of Jurists and Lawyers and various other
groups. Indefatigable, Hirschfeld set about establishing the
Institut des sciences sexologiques in Paris, issuing an international appeal for aid in the journal *Anthropos*. The project
was cut short when Hirschfeld died of heart failure on May 14,
1935--his sixty-seventh birthday.

It may be that many German homosexuals viewed the destruc-
tion of the Berlin Institute as an anti-Semitic act rather than
as an expression of anti-homosexual sentiment. Some could con-
ceivably have approved of the measure, particularly if they were
Nazi sympathizers or male supremacists; Hirschfeld's reform efforts
had long been disparaged in some homosexual circles (see page 49
above). Yet others may have been reconciled by the knowledge that
Hitler's right-hand man, Ernst Röhm, was a homosexual. At the
outset of the Third Reich, it was all too easy to ignore the clear
pronouncements on homosexuality which the Nazi Party had issued.

Appallingly little information is available on the situation of
homosexuals in Nazi Germany. Many historians have hinted darkly
at the unspeakable practices of a Nazi elite supposedly overrun
with perverts, but this charge is both unsubstantiated and insidi-
ous. Upon closer examination, it turns out to be no more than
the standard use of anti-homosexual prejudice to defame any given
individual or group--a practice, incidentally, at which the Nazis
were supreme masters. The fact that homosexuals were major victims
of Nazism is mentioned in only a few of the standard histories of
the period, and those historians who do mention the facts seem
reluctant to dwell on the subject and turn quickly to the fate of
other minorities in Nazi Germany. Yet tens, perhaps hundreds of
thousands of homosexuals were interned in Nazi concentration camps.
They were consigned to the lowest position in the camp hierarchy
and, subjected to abuse by both guards and fellow prisoners, most
of them perished. The few who managed to survive have been reluctant to reveal their experiences, largely because Paragraph 175
remained on the law books in post-war Germany.

The Protestant Church of Austria recently estimated that
220,000 homosexuals were killed during the Third Reich.[6] The
exact number is unknown and will remain so. Although statistics
are available on the number of men brought to trial and convicted
on violations of Paragraph 175 during these years, many more were
sent to camps without the benefit of a trial. Moreover, many
homosexuals were summarily executed by firing squads; this was

Bust of Hirschfeld Carried by Nazis

particularly the case with homosexuals in the military (which included virtually every able-bodied man during the final years of World War II). Finally, many concentration camps systematically destroyed their records when it became apparent that German defeat was imminent.

The indisputable beginning of Nazi terror against homosexuals was marked by the murder of Ernst Röhm on June 28, 1934, "the night of the long knives." Röhm was the man who, in 1919, first made Hitler aware of his own political potential, and the two were close friends for fifteen years. During that time, Röhm rose to SA Chief of Staff, transforming the Brownshirt militia from a handful of hardened goons and embittered ex-soldiers into an effective fighting force some 500,000 strong--the instrument of Nazi terror. Hitler needed Röhm's military skill and could rely upon his personal loyalty, but he was ultimately a pragmatist. As part of a compromise with the Reichswehr leadership, whose support he needed to become Führer, Hitler allowed Göring and Himmler to murder Röhm along with dozens of loyal SA officers. For public relations purposes, and especially to quell the outrage felt in the ranks of the SA, Hitler justified his blatant power play by pointing to Röhm's homosexuality. (A joke immediately arose: "What will he do when he finds out about Goebbel's club foot?"[7]) Hitler, of course, had known about Röhm's homosexuality since 1919, and it had become common knowledge in 1925, when Röhm appeared in court to charge a male prostitute with theft. During these years, the

official policy of the party was unambiguously anti-homosexual,
and many Nazis felt that Röhm discredited the entire party and
should be purged. Hitler, however, was willing to cover up for
him for years—until he stood in the way of larger plans.

As Röhm and his men were being rounded up for the massacre,
the new chief of staff received his first order from Hitler:

> I expect all SA leaders to help preserve and strengthen
> the SA in its capacity as a pure and cleanly institution.
> In particular, I should like every mother to be able to
> allow her son to join the SA, Party, and Hitler Youth
> without fear that he may become morally corrupted in
> their ranks. I therefore require all SA commanders to
> take the utmost pains to ensure that offenses under
> Paragraph 175 are met by immediate expulsion of the
> culprit from the SA and the Party. . . . (8)

Hitler had good reason to be concerned about the reputation of
Nazi organizations, most of which were based upon strict segrega-
tion of the sexes. Hitler Youth, for example, was disparagingly
referred to as Homo Youth throughout the Third Reich, a charac-
terization which the leadership vainly struggled to eliminate.
Indeed, most of the handful of publications on homosexuality which
appeared during the fascist regime were devoted to new and rather
bizarre methods of "detection" and "prevention."[9]

Rudolf Diels, the founder of the Gestapo, recorded some of
Hitler's personal thoughts on the subject:

> He lectured me on the role of homosexuality in history and
> politics. It had destroyed ancient Greece, he said. Once
> rife, it extended its contagious effects like an ineluctable
> law of nature to the best and most manly of characters, eli-
> minating from the reproductive process those very men on
> whose offspring a nation depended. The immediate result
> of the vice was, however, that unnatural passion swiftly

became dominant in public affairs if it were allowed to spread unchecked. (10)

With its mingled elements of condemnation, dread, and admiration, Hitler's view appears to be a concatenation of eugenics, fear of conspiracy (similar to the "Elders of Zion" legend), and the theory of homosexual superiority advanced by Hans Blüher.

The tone had been set by the Röhm Putsch, and on its first anniversary--June 28, 1935--the campaign against homosexuality was escalated by the promulgation of Paragraph 175a, the first revision of Paragraph 175 in its sixty-five-year history. Until 1935, the only punishable offense had been sodomy; under Paragraph 175a, nine possible "acts" were punishable, including a kiss, an embrace, even homosexual fantasies.[11] One man, for instance, was successfully prosecuted on the grounds that he had observed a couple making love in a park and had watched only the man.[12] Under the Nazi legal system, criminal acts were less important in determining guilt than was criminal intent: the "phenomenological" theory of justice claimed to evaluate character, not just deeds.[13] The "healthy sensibility of the people" *(gesundes Volksempfinden)* was elevated to the highest normative legal concept, and the Nazis were thus in a position to prosecute solely on the grounds of sexual orientation. (After World War II, incidentally, this law was immediately stricken from the books in the German Democratic Republic as a product of fascist thinking, but it remained on the books in Federal Republic.[14])

Once Paragraph 175a was in effect, the annual number of

convictions on charges of homosexuality leaped to about ten times
the number in the pre-Nazi period.[15] The law was so loosely formulated that it could be, and was, applied against heterosexuals
whom the Nazis wanted to eliminate. The most notorious example
of an individual convicted on trumped-up charges was General Werner von Fritsch, Army Chief of Staff; and the law was also used
repeatedly against Catholic clergymen. But the law was undoubted-
ly used primarily against homosexuals, and the court system was
aided in the witchhunt by the entire German populace, which was
encouraged to scrutinize the behavior of neighbors and to denounce
suspects to the Gestapo. The number of men convicted on charges
of violating Paragraph 175 during the Nazi period totaled around
50,000:[16]

1933:	853	1938:	8115
1934:	948	1939:	7614
1935:	ca. 3700	1940:	3773
1936:	5321	1941:	3735
1937:	8721	1942:	2678
	1943: 996 (1st quarter)		
	1944-45: ?		

The Gestapo was the agent of the next escalation of the
campaign against homosexuality. Heinrich Himmler, Reichsführer
SS and head of the Gestapo, richly deserves a reputation as the
most fanatically anti-homosexual member of the Nazi leadership.
On October 11, 1936, he gave a speech on the subject of homosexuality and described the murder of Röhm (which he had engineered)
in these terms: "Two years ago. . .when it became necessary, we
did not hesitate to strike this plague with death, even within

our own ranks." Himmler closed with these words:

> Just as we today have gone back to the ancient Germanic
> view on the question of marriage mixing different races,
> so too in our judgment of homosexuality—a symptom of
> degeneracy which could destroy our race—we must return
> to the guiding Nordic principle: extermination of degen-
> erates. Germany stands and falls with the purity of
> the race. (17)

A few months earlier, Himmler had prepared for action by reor-
ganizing the entire state police into three divisions. The political executive, Division II, was directly responsible for the
control of "illegal parties and organizations, leagues and economic groups, reactionaries and the Church, freemasonry, and
homosexuality."18

Himmler personally favored the immediate "extermination of
degenerates," but he was not empowered to order executions. For
the time being, homosexuals were merely required to serve out
their prison sentences (although second offenders were subject
to castration). However, Himmler found a way around this ob-
stacle. Following release from prison, all "enemies of the state"
—including homosexuals—were to be taken into protective custody
and detained indefinitely. "Protective custody" (Schutzhaft) was
a euphemism for concentration camp internment. Himmler gave special
orders that homosexuals be placed in Level 3 camps, human death
mills reserved for Jews and homosexuals. In 1937, Himmler added
a codicil dealing with homosexuals apprehended within the SS:

> After serving the sentence imposed by the court, they will,
> upon my instructions, be taken to a concentration camp and
> there shot while attempting to escape. (19)

The official SS newspaper, *Das Schwarze Korps*, announced in
1937 that there were two million German homosexuals and called
for their internment in concentration camps.[20] The extent to which
Himmler succeeded in this undertaking is unknown, but the number
was far in excess of the 50,000 who served jail sentences. The
Gestapo dispatched hundreds to camps without a trial. Moreover,
"protective custody" was enforced retroactively, so that any homosexual who had ever come to the attention of the police prior to
the Third Reich was subject to immediate internment.[21] (The police
of one Berlin district alone had an index of 30,000 homosexuals in
1940.[22]) And beginning with the *Anschluss* (annexation) of Austria
in 1938, homosexuals from Nazi-occupied countries were also interned
in German camps.[23]

The chances for survival in a Level 3 camp were low indeed.
Homosexuals were distinguished from other prisoners by a pink triangle about three-and-one-half inches high, worn on the left side
of the jacket and on the right trouser leg. To make homosexuals
more readily distinguishable, pink triangles were about an inch
larger than the yellow triangles worn by Jews or red triangles
worn by political prisoners.[24] There was no possibility of "passing" as a heterosexual, and the presence of "marked men" in the
all-male camp population evoked the same reaction as in modern
prisons: homosexuals were brutally assaulted and sexually abused.
One survivor wrote:

> During the first weeks of my imprisonment, I often thought
> I was the only available target on whom everyone was free

to vent his aggressions. Things improved when I was
assigned to a labor detail that worked outside the camp
at Metz, because everything took place in public view.
I was made clerk of the labor detail, which meant that
I worked all day and then looked after the records at
the guardhouse between midnight and two a.m. Because
of this "overtime," I was allowed seconds at lunch—
if any food was left over. This is the fact to which
I probably owe my survival. . . . I saw quite a number
of pink triangles. I don't know how they were eventually
killed. . . . One day they were just gone. (25)

Concentration camp internment served a twofold purpose: the labor

power of prisoners boosted the national economy significantly,

and undesirables could be efficiently liquidated by the simple

expedient of reducing their food rations to slightly below the

subsistence level. One survivor wrote of witnessing "Project

Pink" at his camp:

The homosexuals were grouped into liquidation commandos
and placed under triple camp discipline. That meant less
food, more work, stricter supervision. If a prisoner
with a pink triangle became sick, it spelled his doom.
Admission to the clinic was forbidden. (26)

The first authentic account of concentration camp internment

appeared in the German homophile magazine *Humanitas* in 1954. Its

author was a physician, L. D. Claassen von Neudegg, who had been

imprisoned at Sachsenhausen. These are excerpts from his account:

After roll call on the evening of June 20, 1942, an order
was suddenly given: "All prisoners with the pink triangle
will remain standing at attention!" We stood on the desolate,
broad square, and from somewhere a warm summer breeze carried
the sweet fragrance of resin and wood from the regions of
freedom; but we couldn't savor it, because our throats were
hot and dry from fear. Then the guardhouse door of the com-
mand tower opened, and an SS officer and some of his lackies
strode toward us. Our detail commander barked: "Three hun-
dred criminal deviants, present as ordered!" We were regis-
tered, and then it was revealed to us that in accordance with
an order from the Reichsführung SS, our category was to be put

in an intensified penalty company, and we would be transferred as a unit to the Klinker Brickworks the following morning. The Klinker factory! We shuddered, for the human death mill was more than feared. . . .

Forced to drag along twenty corpses, the rest of us encrusted with blood, we entered the Klinker works.

We had been here for almost two months, but it seemed like endless years to us. When we were "transferred" here, we had numbered around 300 men. Whips were used more frequently each morning, when we were forced down into the clay pits under the wailing of the camp sirens. "Only fifty are still alive," whispered the man next to me. "Stay in the middle--then you won't get hit so much."

. . . .

The escapees had been brought back. "Homo" was scrawled scornfully across their clothing for their last march through the camp. To increase their thirst, they were forced to eat oversalted food, and then they were placed on the block and whipped. Afterwards, drums were hung around their necks, which they to beat while shouting, "Hurrah, we're back!" The three men were hanged.

. . . .

Summer, 1944. One morning there was an eruption of restlessness among the patients of the hospital barracks where I worked. Fear and uncertainty had arisen from rumors about new measures on the part of the SS hospital administration. At the administration's order, the courier of the political division had requisitioned certain medical records, and now he was arriving at the camp for delivery. Fever charts shot up; the sick were seized with a gnawing fear. After a few days, the awful mystery of the records was solved. Experiments had been ordered involving living subjects and phosphorus: methods of treating phosphorus burns were to be developed and tested. I must be silent about the effects of this series of experiments, which proceeded with unspeakable pain, fear, blood, and tears, for it is impossible to put the misery into words. (27)

Four years after the publication of Neudegg's account, the West German *Institut für Zeitgeschichte* (Institute of Modern History) issued the autobiographical jottings of Rudolf Höss, adjutant and commander of the concentration camps at Sachsenhausen and, later, Auschwitz. They verify Neudegg's account in many details; these are the words of Höss:

At Sachsenhausen, the homosexuals were segregated in a
special section as a matter of course. They were also
put to work separately from the other prisoners. They
worked in the clay pits of the Klinker Works. It was
hard work, and each one had to produce a definite quota.
They were continually exposed to the elements, for a
certain number of loads had to be delivered daily. The
kiln work could not be interrupted because of a lack of
raw materials, so they simply had to work regardless of
weather, summer and winter. . . .

While those willing to change, those who had the strong
will for it, were also able to withstand the hardest work,
the others slowly fell apart at a rate that depended upon
individual constitution. Since they could not or would
not give up their vice, they knew they would never be
released. This extremely powerful psychological factor
hastened the physical collapse of these individuals, who
usually had a frail constitution. If one lost his "friend"
through sickness or death, you could see it was all over.
Many committed suicide. The "friend" meant everything to
these creatures in this situation. On several occasions
two friends committed suicide together. (28)

But the death of other pink triangles was more brutal. Another

survivor gave this account:

. . . He was a young and healthy man. The first evening's
roll call after he was added to our penal company was his
last. When he arrived, he was seized and ridiculed, then
beaten and kicked, and finally spat upon. He suffered
alone and in silence. Then they put him under a cold
shower. It was a frosty winter evening, and he stood
outside the barracks all through that long, bitterly cold
night. When morning came, his breathing had become an
audible rattle. Bronchial pneumonia was later given as
the cause of his death. But before it had come to that,
he was again beaten and kicked. Then he was tied to a
post and placed under an arc lamp until he began to sweat,
again put under a cold shower, and so on. He died toward
evening. (29)

This was the practice in the concentration camps at Sachsensenhausen,

Natzweiler, Fühlsbüttel, Neusustrum, Sonnenburg, Dachau, Lichten-

burg, Mauthausen, Ravensbrück, Neuengamme, Grossrosen--camps where

homosexuals are known to have been interned.[30] In the final months of the war, the men with pink triangles received brief military training: they were to be sent out as cannon fodder in the last-ditch defense of the fatherland. The ruthlessness of the Nazis culminated in actions so perversely vindictive as to be almost incomprehensible. Ten youths arrested for stealing coal at a railroad station were taken into protective custody and duly placed in a concentration camp. Shocked that such innocent boys were forced to sleep in a barracks also occupied by pink triangles, the SS guards chose what must have seemed to them the lesser of two evils: they took the youths aside and gave them fatal injections of morphine.[31] Morality was saved.

The self-righteousness that could prompt this type of action cuts through the entire ideology glorifying racial purity and extermination of degenerates to reveal stark fear of homosexuality. Something of this fear was echoed in the statement of Hitler cited above, so different in its tone from the propagandistic cant of Himmler's exhortations. While Himmler saw homosexuals as congenital cowards and weaklings, Hitler could at least imagine them as "the best and the most manly of characters"--and therefore as especially threatening. With their relentless emphasis upon strength, purity, cleanliness, and masculine comradeship, the Nazi *Männerbünde* (all-male groups) surely contained a strong element of deeply repressed homoeroticism; the degree of repression was evidenced by the vehemence of the Nazi reaction to those who were overtly homosexual. The biblical scapegoat was the sacrificial animal upon whose head the amorphous guilt of the entire community was placed. Homosexuals served precisely this function in the Third Reich.

The ideological rationale for homosexual genocide was quite another matter. According to the doctrine of social Darwinism, only the fittest were meant to survive, and the law of the jungle was the final arbiter of human history. If the Germans were destined to become the master race by virtue of inherent biological superiority, the breeding stock could only be improved by the removal of, to use Friedländer's word, *Kümmerlinge*. A system of ranking women according to the number of their offspring was devised by Minister of the Interior Wilhelm Frick, who demanded that homosexuals "be hunted down mercilessly, for their vice can only lead to the demise of the German people."[32] Himmler recounted to his SS generals the ancient Germanic mode of execution for homosexuals --drowning in bogs--and added: "That was no punishment, merely the extinction of an abnormal life. It had to be removed just as we pull up stinging nettles, toss them on a heap and burn them."[33]

There is a certain affinity between the "third sex" ideology of Ulrichs and Hirschfeld and the biologistic argument for homosexual genocide advanced by Himmler. Both turned on the idea that homosexuals are congenitally different from either men or women; but if this, for the Scientific-Humanitarian Committee, was a reason for arguing that homosexuals should be accepted on the same basis as the two other sexes, it was for the Nazis sufficient grounds for extermination. It is interesting to note that Himmler was at

one time an animal breeder (actually a chicken farmer) and thus
perhaps predisposed to find a "third sex" worse than useless.
Hitler, on the other hand, was the Nazi visionary and an erstwhile
artist; and there is a truly striking affinity between his views
on homosexuality and those of Friedländer and Blüher. These male
supremacists wanted to create a new Hellas peopled by strong, naked,
but chaste men, inspired by heroism and capable of leadership.
But the elitism of the Community of the Special (Gemeinschaft der
Eigenen) posed a threat to the folk community (Volksgemeinschaft)
sought by the Nazis; it was a state within a state. It is a com-
monplace to observe that progressive ideas of the pre-Nazi era
were assimilated and transformed into their very opposites by the
Nazis; this supplanting of a positive value by its negative over
time has been termed the dialectic of enlightenment.[32]

Although the Nazi policy on homosexuality can be interpreted
both ideologically and psychologically, in terms of conscious and
subconscious processes, it must also be seen against the background
of the social and sexual revolution which had transformed Germany
during the preceding decades. Modernization had come so quickly
and had produced such glaring contradictions that by 1929, the situation could only be brought under control by making a great leap
forward--or back. The Nazis carried out a "conservative revolution"
which attempted to restore the discipline, the community, and the
morality of a bygone era. For twelve years the clock was stopped;
but history has shown that time was on the side of the homosexual
emancipation movement and other movements for social progress.

NOTES

1. Kurt Hiller, *Leben gegen die Zeit*, vol. 1, *Logos* (Reinbek bei Hamburg: Rowohlt, 1969), pp. 226-294.

2. Rudolf Klare, *Homosexualität und Strafrecht* (Hamburg: Hanseatische Verlagsanstalt, 1937), p. 30.

3. World Committee for the Victims of Fascism, *Brown Book of the Hitler Terror* (New York: Alfred A. Knopf, 1933), p. 158.

4. *Ibid.*, pp. 158-161.

5. *Anthropos* I/2 (1934) 1 (= *Medical Review of Reviews* # 460).

6. Reported in *Gay Liberator* #41 (November 1974), p. 3.

7. Richard Grunberger, *The Twelve-Year Reich: A Social History of Nazi Germany 1933-1945* (New York: Ballantine, 1972), p. 366.

8. Hans Peter Bleuel, *Strength through Joy: Sex and Society in Nazi Germany*, transl. J. Maxwell Brownjohn (London: Secker & Warburg, 1973), p. 219.

9. See, e.g., Germany, Luftwaffe, *Anweisung für Truppenärzte zur Beurteilung gleichgeschlechtlicher Handlungen* (Berlin: n.p., 1944) and Werner Gauhl, *Gleichgeschlechtliche Handlungen Jugendlicher: Statistische Untersuchungen über Gruppenbildung bei Jugendlichen. . . .* (Darmstadt: n.p., 1940).

10. Bleuel, *op. cit.*, p. 218.

11. The categories were developed by Johannes Nägler and published in his *Der Tatbestand der sogenannten widernatürlichen Unzucht*; they are reprinted in Klare, *op. cit.*, p. 135.

12. Wolfgang Harthauser, "Der Massenmord an Homosexuellen im Dritten Reich," *Das grosse Tabu: Zeugnisse und Dokumente zum Problem der Homosexualität*, ed. Willhart Schlegel (Munich: Rütten & Loening, 1967), p. 20.

13. Grunberger, *op. cit.*, pp. 133-134.

14. Cf. Harry Wilde (i.e., Harry Schulze-Wilde), *Das Schicksal der Verfemten: Die Verfolgung der Homosexuellen im "Dritten Reich" und ihre Stellung in der heutigen Gesellschaft* (Tübingen:

Katzmann, 1969), p. 62.

15. A table of charges and convictions for the years 1882 to 1933 appears in Klare, *op. cit.*, pp. 144-145.

16. Cf. Bleuel, *op. cit.*, pp. 212-213, and Harthauser, *op. cit.*, p. 20.

17. Wilde, *op. cit.*, p. 36.

18. Harthauser, *op. cit.*, p. 23.

19. Bleuel, *op. cit.*, p. 223.

20. Karl August Eckhardt, "Das sind Staatsfeinde!", *Das Schwarze Korps* III/9 (March 4, 1937) 1-2. Cf. also his "Widernatürliche Unzucht ist todeswürdig," *ibid.*, I/12 (May 22, 1935) 13.

21. On retrospective legislation, see Grunberger, *op. cit.*, p. 133.

22. Wilde, *op. cit.*, p. 30.

23. The one book-length account of concentration camp internment is by an Austrian: Heinz Heger, *Die Männer mit dem rosa Winkel* (Hamburg: Merlin, 1972).

24. *Ibid.*, p. 33.

25. Harthauser, *op. cit.*, pp. 30-31.

26. *Ibid.*, p. 32.   27. *Ibid.*, pp. 9-10, 11-13.

28. Wilde, *op. cit.*, pp. 27-28.

29. Harthauser, *op. cit.*, p. 32.

30. *Ibid.*, pp. 26-27.

31. Wilde, *op. cit.*, pp. 37-38.

32. Harthauser, *op. cit.*, p. 13.

33. Bleuel, *op. cit.*, p. 221.

34. Max Horkheimer and Theodor W. Adorno, *Dialektik der Aufklärung* (Amsterdam: Querido Verlag, 1947).

HOMOSEXUALITY

Lesbians and Gay Men
in Society, History and Literature

Acosta, Mercedes de. **Here Lies The Heart.** 1960

Bannon, Ann. **I Am a Woman.** 1959

Bannon, Ann. **Journey To a Woman.** 1960

Bannon, Ann. **Odd Girl Out.** 1957

Bannon, Ann. **Women in The Shadows.** 1959

Barney, Natalie Clifford. **Aventures de L'Esprit.** 1929

Barney, Natalie Clifford. **Traits et Portraits.** 1963

Brooks, Romaine. **Portraits, Tableaux, Dessins.** 1952

Carpenter, Edward. **Intermediate Types Among Primitive Folk.** 1919

Casal, Mary. **The Stone Wall.** 1930

Cory, Donald Webster. **The Homosexual in America.** 1951

Craigin, Elisabeth. **Either Is Love.** 1937

Daughters of Bilitis. **The Ladder.** Volumes I - XVI. Including an **Index To The Ladder** by Gene Damon. 1956 - 1972. Nine vols.

Documents of the Homosexual Rights Movement in Germany, 1836 - 1927. 1975

Ellis, Havelock and John Addington Symonds. **Sexual Inversion.** 1897

Fitzroy, A. T. **Despised and Rejected.** 1917

Ford, Charles and Parker Tyler. **The Young and Evil.** 1933

Frederics, Diana. **Diana: A Strange Autobiography.** 1939

Friedlaender, Benedict. **Renaissance des Eros Uranios.** 1904

A Gay Bibliography. 1975

A Gay News Chronology, 1969 - May, 1975. 1975

Gordon, Mary. **Chase of the Wild Goose.** 1936

Government Versus Homosexuals. 1975

Grosskurth, Phyllis. **John Addington Symonds.** 1964

Gunn, Peter. **Vernon Lee: Violet Paget, 1856 - 1935.** 1964

A Homosexual Emancipation Miscellany, c. 1835 - 1952. 1975

Karsch-Haack, F[erdinand]. **Das Gleichgeschlechtliche Leben der Naturvölker.** 1911

Katz, Jonathan. **Coming Out!** 1975

Lesbianism and Feminism in Germany, 1895 - 1910. 1975

Lind, Earl. **Autobiography of an Androgyne.** 1918

Lind, Earl. **The Female-Impersonators.** 1922

Loeffler, Donald L. **An Analysis of the Treatment of the Homosexual Character in Dramas Produced in the New York Theatre From 1950 to 1968.** 1975

Mallet, Françoise. **The Illusionist.** 1952

Miss Marianne Woods and Miss Jane Pirie Against Dame Helen Cumming Gordon. 1811 - 1819

Mattachine Society. **Mattachine Review.** Volumes I - XIII. 1955 - 1966. Six vols.

Mayne, Xavier. **Imre: A Memorandum.** 1908

Mayne, Xavier. **The Intersexes.** 1908

Morgan, Claire. **The Price of Salt.** 1952

Niles, Blair. **Strange Brother.** 1931

Olivia. **Olivia.** 1949

Rule, Jane. **The Desert of the Heart.** 1964

Sagarin, Edward. **Structure and Ideology in an Association of Deviants.** 1975

Steakley, James D. **The Homosexual Emancipation Movement in Germany.** 1975

Sturgeon, Mary C. **Michael Field.** 1921

Sutherland, Alistair and Patrick Anderson. **Eros: An Anthology of Friendship.** 1961

Sweet, Roxanna Thayer. **Political and Social Action in Homophile Organizations.** 1975

Tobin, Kay and Randy Wicker. **The Gay Crusaders.** 1972

Ulrichs, Carl Heinrich. **Forschungen Über Das Rätsel Der Mannmännlichen Liebe.** 1898

Underwood, Reginald. **Bachelor's Hall.** 1937

[Vincenzo], Una, Lady Troubridge. **The Life of Radclyffe Hall.** 1963

Vivien, Renée **Poèmes de Renée Vivien.** Two vols. in one. 1923/24

Weirauch, Anna Elisabet. **The Outcast.** 1933

Weirauch, Anna Elisabet. **The Scorpion.** 1932

Wilhelm, Gale. **Torchlight to Valhalla.** 1938

Wilhelm, Gale. **We Too Are Drifting.** 1935

Winsloe, Christa. **The Child Manuela.** 1933